"When I heard that Mandy Ellis was writing a book about leading with literacy in schools, my first thoughts were: 'It's about time,' and 'I can't wait to read it!' *Lead with Literacy* takes you, the reader, on a walk through hallways and classrooms while sharing an engaging narrative of how literacy must be passionately instilled in all children. The countless beautiful treasures found in this book will help new and seasoned educators chart a course filled with engaging, creative, and fun ideas to help you *Lead with Literacy*!"

—**Sue Tonnesen,** elementary principal, SD62,
Sooke, British Columbia, Canada, @suetonnesen

"*Lead with Literacy* invites you on a journey to create a map toward building and embedding a vibrant and joyful reading culture in any school. The multitude of ideas, experiences, and adventures shared by Mandy, her school, and her PLN give the readers unlimited resources and inspiration to help make their own school's mission and vision come to life. Mandy's emotional journey and passion for reading are truly painted with words as she helps her readers strengthen their identity, reflect on their learning, and share their own story with others. This book is a treasure for any educator who wishes to continue to embody the PIRATE leadership with love of reading at the forefront. As a teacher and leader, I am going back to my classroom energized, engaged, and passionate about empowering students and readers through words, stories, books, and community. I embrace her challenge and commit to 'read for fun, read for learning, but, most of all, read to lead.'"

—**Roman Nowak,** teacher/student success leader/agent
of transformation, *CSDCEO*, Ontario, Canada, @NowakRo

"Anyone in education needs to read *Lead with Literacy*. Mandy is, in my opinion, one of the leading experts in our country on how to build a literacy culture at a school, and she lives this out each and every day. With fun stories, amazing examples, and creative ideas, you'll be wanting more as you turn each page of this book. What a literary gem and a must-read!"

—**Adam Welcome,** director of innovation and technology, Principal of
the Year, coauthor of *Kids Deserve It!,* @awelcome

"*Lead with Literacy* gives administrators and teachers valuable nuggets of knowledge to cultivate an environment of young readers. Through reflection questions and ideas for implementation, Ellis merges her love of reading with her love of kids and encourages all educators to do the same."

—**Lindsy Stumpenhorst,** elementary principal, @principalboots

"Finally! This is *the* book to ignite literacy in our schools! Mandy's passion and enthusiasm for reading come through loud and clear in *Lead with Literacy.* As her colleague, I know firsthand how passionate Mandy is as a lead learner. Her school has taken significant steps to get students and staff excited about reading. If you're looking for practical ideas to infuse literacy into your school in creative ways, this is your book! It'll leave students and staff wanting more and is a must-read for all teachers and school leaders who truly want to develop and transform their school into a culture of readers!"

—**Greg Fairchild,** principal,
Banner Elementary School, @gjfairchild, @BESBobcats

"Leaders are readers, plain and simple. Show me a school that is moving forward and I will show you a school leader that loves to read and has instilled that same love in others. In this book, Mandy Ellis draws from her experience as the lead reader in her school to help you create a culture in your school that will influence your students, teachers, parents, and community members to love to read."

—**Jason Leahy,** executive director,
Illinois Principals Association, @IPA_Jason

"*Lead with Literacy* is more than a book; it is a call to action. Throughout the pages, Mandy Ellis does a marvelous job of inspiring readers to want to do more when it comes to literacy in our schools. Not only does she offer advice, she gives real-life examples of how to improve literacy for yourself and for an entire school building. This is a must-read!"

—**Ryan Sheehy,** principal, speaker, and
author of *Be the One for Kids,* @sheehyrw

"Mandy Ellis's approach outlined in *Lead with Literacy* can be described as 'premiere, an all-in approach, a championship mindset for educating kids, cutting edge, and innovation at its finest!' This book outlines a vision for educators that can lead to a full transformation in the entire philosophy related to promoting, highlighting, and engaging the entire school community in literacy and learning. If you are interested in creating a top-notch culture of literacy and learning in your school district, this is a can't-miss book!"

—**Dr. Matt Gordon**, superintendent, Rankin School, @drmgordon

"Mandy has passionately written a masterpiece with her book, *Lead with Literacy*. Her words are a MUST for every principal/educator who truly cares about the literacy life of his/her students and school community. It was an honor to read through this piece of art, as I felt her passion on every page."

—**Shelli L. Nafziger**, EdD, K–4 principal,
Germantown Hills School District, @drshelli

"*Lead with Literacy* is the treasure map you need to empower your school community on its journey to create a culture of readers. Mandy Ellis challenges educators to remember what it feels like to get lost in a book and to continuously promote the love of reading. Begin this call to action today, and you won't be disappointed!"

—**Stefanie Pitzer,** instructional technology coach,
Dunlap School District #323, @stefaniepitzer

"*Lead with Literacy* is a must-have book for any school/principal/teacher looking for intentional and fun literacy engagement strategies for students and families. Mandy's book provides practical and easy ideas to implement for all schools. I have followed her for years on social media, using her ideas daily! I am always eagerly awaiting anything new from her. But promoting literacy is her strength. If you are committed to creating a literacy rich environment for your school, this is the book for you."

—**Melinda Miller**, principal, Willard East Elementary, @mmiller7571

"*Lead with Literacy* is a must-read for all school leaders and educators! You will find a variety of ideas of how you can make literacy a priority on your school campus. You can read sections of this book and implement strategies the following day! *Lead with Literacy* is so much more than just about having books on campus. It's about the impact books and literacy can have on a school culture and the relationships with students that can be built around literacy. *Lead with Literacy* will definitely be a book I will be gifting my staff and colleagues with!"

—**Jessica Gomez,** principal,
Colton Joint Unified School District, @jgomezprincipal

"This book had my mind racing! In *Lead with Literacy,* Mandy Ellis shares an inspiring vision of how our schools can foster readers. This book isn't designed to make our students just like reading but to create a culture that truly loves and embraces reading. This book gives amazing ideas to get all of the stakeholders in the school community excited and eager to be part of that culture. Through events, contests, and a full immersion of reading opportunities, this read, regardless of your position, will drive you and those around you to want to develop a true culture of readers as well as give you incredible ideas on how to do so."

—**John Wawczak,** principal,
Covington Elementary School, @MrWawczak

"As a reluctant reader, I always found an excuse for not picking up a book. There was always a game to play, a show to watch, or squirrel that ran by, all taking me away from diving in and spending time in a story. That didn't change when I took a leadership position. There was always something else to do. But as leaders we need to know and understand that eyes are on us all the time. What we model is what we get. *Lead with Literacy* provides the why and the how for taking your school to a different level with literacy instruction."

—**Joe Sanfelippo,** superintendent, author, @joe_sanfelippo

A **LEAD** Like a **PIRATE** *Guide*

LEAD With

LITERACY

A PIRATE Leader's Guide
to Developing a Culture of Readers

Mandy Ellis

LEAD with LITERACY
© 2018 by Mandy Ellis

This book is available at special discounts when purchased in quantity for use as premiums, promotions, fundraisers, or for educational use. For inquiries and details, contact the publisher at books@daveburgessconsulting.com.

Published by Dave Burgess Consulting, Inc.
San Diego, CA
DaveBurgessConsulting.com

Cover Design by Genesis Kohler
Editing and Interior Design by My Writers' Connection

Library of Congress Control Number: 2018942304
Paperback ISBN: 978-1-946444-81-3
Ebook ISBN: 978-1-946444-82-0

First Printing: June 2018

Contents

Foreword by Beth Houf and Shelley Burgess xi

Lead Like a PIRATE xiii

My Story xv

SECTION I: BE THE LEAD READER 1

Chapter 1: Create a Culture of Readers 3

Chapter 2: Spark a Love of Books 7

Chapter 3: Read by Example 11

SECTION II: SET SAILWITH STUDENTS 23

Chapter 4: Student Choice 27

Chapter 5: Ample Access 33

Chapter 6: Independent Reading Time 43

Chapter 7: Learning Environment 49

SECTION III: READ. CONNECT. REPEAT. 57

Chapter 8: Build Relationships with Books 59

Chapter 9: Treasure the Risks and Rewards of
Setting Big Goals 77

Chapter 10: Equip Your Crew to Be Reader Leaders 93

Chapter 11: Encourage Reading at Home,
on the Go, *Everywhere!* 109

Chapter 12: Get Enthusiastic about Reading! 121

Concluding Thoughts:
Lead the Way to Reading Treasure 133

Bibliography 135

Acknowledgments 137

Bring Mandy Ellis to Your School or District 139

More from Dave Burgess Consulting, Inc. 140

About the Author 153

FOREWORD

by Beth Houf and Shelley Burgess

The life of an educational leader can be a lonely road. Your task list has multiplied, yet time seems to have diminished. It is essential that you have a strong network of support to celebrate the great things happening—as well as get you through those rough moments.

We wrote *Lead Like a PIRATE* to do just that. We wanted to help support educators by sharing our stories and strategies. We wanted to be sure that no one felt as if she/he were alone. Our goal has been to set up systems of support through our PLN to empower leaders to take risks to ensure that school is an amazing place for students *and* staff.

Since our book's release, it has been inspiring to watch our #LeadLAP crew grow. The examples and stories shared daily on our hashtag are encouraging beyond belief. We came to realize that we are surrounded by greatness—and that greatness needed a voice.

One evening after our book was published, we started brainstorming how we could continue to support leaders in a way that wasn't the norm. One thing we discussed was that leaders sometimes feel overwhelmed by the amount of information available and the speed at which it comes at them. We asked, "How might we offer bite-size expertise for leaders that would have huge impact on schools?" Our answer was the *Lead Like a PIRATE Guides*.

When we wrote *Lead Like a PIRATE*, one of things we wanted to convey is our firm belief that PIRATE leaders are never satisfied—they relentlessly search for new and better ways to make school amazing for students, staff, parents, and communities. They lead with passion and a palpable enthusiasm that radiates within the walls and around the campus. Mandy Ellis is this type of leader, and Dunlap Grade School (DGS) benefits greatly because she brings her passion for reading and literacy to work with her Every. Single. Day.

As educators, we all understand the need to implement high-quality literacy programs in our schools, and we all support literacy in a variety of ways. Mandy takes her role as a leader of literacy to the next level as she works diligently to infuse reading into every aspect of her school's culture. From the moment you walk through the doors of DGS, and as you move through the halls, into the cafeteria, onto the playground, stop into the classrooms, or visit a staff meeting, the message is clear: Reading is treasured here.

In her *Lead Like a PIRATE Guide*, *Lead with Literacy*, Mandy pushes open the doors of her school and walks you through the steps she has taken to make literacy come alive. From the "bathtub of books" to the #BookShelfie Station and a dog named Teddy, Mandy shares many impactful, yet easy-to-implement, ways to make reading a priority in *your* school, many of which you can start next week! In true PIRATE fashion, Mandy's sense of purpose, passion, and priorities has created a ripple effect in her school and community. With a little effort, some creativity, a lot of energy, and a ton of enthusiasm, Mandy has transformed her school into an amazing place. We are honored to have her as part of our crew and thrilled to bring you her *Lead Like a PIRATE Guide: Lead with Literacy*.

LEAD LIKE A PIRATE

Passion

Pirate leaders bring their passion to work. They also work to identify and bring out the passions of their staff members and students.

Immersion

Pirate leaders are immersed in their work and relationships, which enables them to make an impact on those they lead.

Rapport

Pirate leaders intentionally build trust and rapport with the entire crew.

Ask and Analyze

Pirate leaders ask great questions and engage in meaningful conversations that empower people to take risks.

Transformation

Pirate leaders transform the mundane into the spectacular. They make essentials, such as staff meetings and professional development training, engaging and effective.

Enthusiasm

Pirate leaders are enthusiastic and positive. They work to create an environment where teachers and students are excited about coming to school each day.

MY STORY

Books are lighthouses erected in the great sea of time.
—E.P. Whipple

Somewhere along the line, you became a reader. And now, you have chosen to read this book because you want to be a better leader of reading in your own school or classroom. You want to be the spark in a child's life that engulfs them in the love of learning and reading. So welcome and congratulations! I am so thankful and proud that you are joining me in this lifelong journey of learning.

I am a practicing principal and, like you, I am passionate about instilling a love of literacy and reading in children. Developing reading skills can be a complex process. Students emerge from pre-reading skills in phonics to developing fluency and comprehension skills. Learning to read—and teaching students to read—isn't always easy, which is why the most important tenet of developing a culture of reading in your school is to *foster a love of reading.*

To do that, our children need leaders who promote and love literacy. They need educators who understand that reading is more about building relationships between the text and the reader than it is about the content. Our schools need educators who know our students as readers. We need educators who are growing as readers themselves. We need educators who can teach, lead, and *read* like pirates.

That's what this book is about. Its purpose isn't to teach you specific skills or strategies for individual classroom lessons that are important to develop phonics, phonemic awareness, vocabulary, fluency, and comprehension. The intent of this book is to provide practical and actionable ideas and strategies to deeply embed books, reading, and literacy into the fabric of your school culture. It is my hope that you will find treasures in this book that you can share with the teachers in your school—ideas that they can easily and quickly apply in classrooms. This book is intended to inspire and support you as a school leader to implement strategies that serve as wraparound approaches to develop a school culture of reading.

My true mission is to ensure that more students have ample access to books with no strings attached and that they see the adults in their lives as strong models of literacy and as lifelong learners.

SECTION I

BE THE LEAD READER

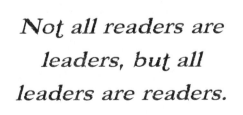

Not all readers are leaders, but all leaders are readers.

−Harry S. Truman

In this section, we'll look at a few of the ways you can develop a culture of reading, specifically as it relates to your example as the lead learner of your school.

Every school has a culture. The culture is a direct reflection of the leadership of that school. In his book, *Culturize*, Jimmy Casas reiterates the importance of modeling and stresses that "what you model is what you get." As a leader, staff, students, and families must see you as a reader. When principals serve as instructional leaders or lead learners, reading is an essential component of that role.

Lead Readers share many common characteristics. I encourage you to develop these traits:

- Take ownership and personal accountability for ensuring literacy is embedded in all facets of the school community and learning environment.
- Maintain a professional focus on learning best practices in literacy and sharing those with staff.
- Build relationships with staff and students over books and reading.
- Use daily opportunities to expand a culture of reading in the school setting.
- Continuously read and add books to their professional library.
- Have a strong understanding of current and classic children's literature.
- Provide opportunities for staff and students to share about books in authentic and meaningful ways.
- Support literacy development through allocating resources in intentional and specific ways.

We shouldn't teach great books, we
should teach the love of reading.
—B.F. Skinner

CREATE A CULTURE OF READERS

*Focus can be difficult to master, but as PIRATE
leaders it is critical that we help our teams find that
one thing that needs our attention every single day.*
—Lead Like a PIRATE

A cornerstone school goal in my K–5 elementary school is *"to create a culture of readers."* No matter the year, no matter the initiative, this goal remains constant. The reason is simple: Reading is essential to any profession and is the basis for developing habits of continuous learning. Readers are the ones who will comprise the next generation of scientists, computer programmers, medical professionals, artists, educators, and leaders in every profession. Our job, then, is to ensure that our students become readers.

Like any school improvement plan, reading improvement and achievement is quantified with action steps, data, and statistics, but reading is also woven into the fabric of our school culture. My concern is more with evidence of student learning and engagement than it is with so-called data. Students are more than just Lexile scores and reading levels. More so than the data, I am concerned our teachers match students with books that inspire them. My hope is that the stories students read will prompt them to pick up the next in the series and motivate them to keep reading. I want to see and hear students talking about books, sharing their reactions to the text, and recommending books to their peers. When this communication occurs, reading moves beyond assignments, grades, tasks, and chores. Reading develops a community and happens for the fun of it.

In my school, we monitor progress through assessments, charts, graphs, and in professional learning communities. We want to ensure our students are growing academically and in many ways, and assessment data provides meaningful insight. More importantly, we want kids, regardless of what reading level they come into our school at, to develop a love of reading. This does not come through testing and curriculum but from establishing a culture where students have choice, access, and ability to read and connect with books.

I strongly believe that what we cherish, value, and nurture is what will grow, develop, and flourish. Our staff is well-versed in the standards and best practices related to teaching phonics, phonemic awareness, vocabulary, comprehension, and fluency; evaluating assessment data; and providing differentiated instruction based on student needs. But we do more than that to develop a *culture* of reading:

We talk about books.

We let kids talk about books.

We invest time in learning about the reading habits and lives of our students.

We share our reading lives with our students.

We share book recommendations with each other.

We match students with books that are good fit—those that are both instructionally appropriate but that also reflect their interests and choices.

We celebrate books and readers.

We take risks.

We consider how the physical environment plays a vital role in nurturing learning.

We put books in the hands of our students in numerous ways.

We ensure what we say we value in our mission and vision is truly at the epicenter of our work with our students.

We read.

Children should learn that reading is pleasure, not just something that teachers make you do in school.
—Beverly Cleary

Reflect on Your School's Reading Culture

Leadership Treasure Hunt
(Find This)

When a student or parent comes into the school, what is the first thing they'll see that promotes a love of reading?

Navigating the Seas
(Think About This)

Take the pulse of your school or classroom reading culture. What words would you use to describe how students and staff feel about being a reader in your school or classroom?

Charting the Course
(Take Action)

What elements of your school or classroom culture support or hinder the love of literacy in students and staff?

Share your thoughts and ideas!
#LeadLAP

SPARK A LOVE OF BOOKS

*Pirate leaders want to make a significant difference. They
have a clear vision about where they want to go and why
it is an important journey for people to take with them.*
—Lead Like a PIRATE

I sat in a fourth-grade classroom in the 1990s with the ability, but limited motivation, to read. My test scores showed I
was fluent and could comprehend text, but I was far from a
reader. Despite a house with ample access to books and parents who
supported my education, I was not a reader. Like many students, I
read to get the grade I needed but did not enjoy independent reading.
With too many novel study packets, little choice in what I read, and
round-robin reading, I became increasingly frustrated and agitated
with reading.

That is, until one amazing teacher introduced me to the notion
that the emotion elicited through reading could change your soul. She
first connected and built relationships with her students. We were all

affectionately known as her *poopsies*. Then she turned us on to reading by pushing us as students to connect with books and authors and build the same relationships with the text. Her name was Mrs. Sandra Fiantago, and her investment in my reading life changed the compass on my journey as a reader. It has been more than twenty years, and I still remember seeing tears in my teacher's eyes as she read the final chapters of books like, *Where the Red Fern Grows* by Wilson Rawls and *Bridge to Terabithia* by Karen Patterson. There were no study guides. No tests. No comprehension quizzes. Just raw emotion and deep connection with the characters and their stories. In that class, I became a reader.

Over the course of my formal education, my reading life ebbed and flowed as I encountered books, teachers, and hurdles that hindered my love of reading. I didn't make an emotional connection with some books; some classrooms prohibited collaboration and conversation regarding the text, and some assignments and projects hindered the progress of the actual reading of the book, unnecessarily dragging it out. I became frustrated when teachers took six weeks to read a novel that I wanted to read in six hours. I distinctly remember a teacher extinguishing any desire or passion for reading our class novel by telling me *not* to read ahead. Packets of worksheets asking literal comprehension questions made reading a chore rather than the treasure hunt it should have been.

I don't blame teachers who have made missteps to extinguish a reading spark or who have failed to light a fire for the readers in their classrooms in the past. I truly feel the vast majority of teachers enter the profession with a deep desire to instill a love of learning in their students. Unfortunately, that mission all too often gets lost in the textbooks, study guides, and outdated strategies.

We have to see the bigger picture. Building a culture of readers isn't something that happens when one group of students loves books and the next group of students dreads reading. **We build a culture of readers by establishing a school-wide learning community where students have equal access and opportunity to books, activities, adult models of readers, and reinforcement of the value of reading, regardless of the teacher.**

In my own journey as a student, some educators sparked my love of reading by introducing me to books that made me hungry to read. These teachers motivated me with new book suggestions, prompted me to challenge myself with a new genre, and encouraged me to lose myself in stories that were woven so delicately and seamlessly that they took me to another world. Those are the teachers who made me want to read more, and those are the kinds of experiences all students deserve.

There are many little ways to enlarge your child's world. Love of books is best of all.
—Jacqueline Kennedy Onassis

Reflect on Being a PIRATE Reader

Leadership Treasure Hunt
(Find This)

Make a list of the books that have made lasting emotional connections to your life.

Navigating the Seas
(Think About This)

What type of reader were you in school? How did those experiences as a student shape you as an adult reader?

Charting the Course
(Take Action)

What former educator impacted you as a reader by being a beacon of light to shine the power of text in your life? Have you told them about the impact they had on your life as an educator? Send them a note of appreciation.

Share your thoughts and ideas!
#LeadLAP

READ BY EXAMPLE

*Be relentless in seeking out and
nurturing each person's greatness.*
—Lead Like a PIRATE

I f you were to see my school, my home office, my nightstand, or my iBooks library, you would instantly know that books are an important part of my life. I surround myself with books and magazines. I read articles, books, Twitter posts, and journals voraciously. My focus is both on professional reading and books for personal joy. In some seasons of my life, I read more frequently and can devour multiple books in a week (or day). Even when life gets busy and it takes me longer to finish a single book, reading is still a daily part of my life. That needs to be true for all educators.

"What is the last book you've read that has impacted you as an educator?" When that question was posed at a professional development session, I had to stop and think. I'd read so many, it was hard to choose just one. But as we went around the room, it was clear that wasn't the case for everyone. One teacher even said, "I don't read, and I tell my students that."

I was speechless. (I might have even gasped.)

Not all educators share a passion for reading and learning, but I believe that *must* change if we are going to develop a culture of reading in our schools.

My teaching heart aches when I hear another educator share they don't read or don't have a favorite book. We all have the same number of hours and minutes in a day, and we choose to spend them on the activities that we value. We *must* value reading. If we as leaders and educators aren't serving as strong models of lifelong reading, we cannot expect our students to become readers; they will follow our example far more readily than they will heed our words.

In addition to serving as models for our students and staff, leaders and educators should be reading to stay current on new and best practices, leadership principles, strategies, and teaching techniques. Workshops, conferences, and webinars offered sporadically throughout the year are great, but they can't provide the instant and ongoing infusion of professional development that you can gain by tapping into a book.

When interviewing teaching candidates, I almost always ask, "What book has inspired you to do the work of a teacher?" If they don't have a clear answer, it indicates an attitude that reading and lifelong learning are not innately important to their role as educators. This type of attitude is inconsistent with our school's mission to create a culture of readers. Being a reader and being able to share what you are currently reading demonstrates an inherent belief that you are a lifelong learner.

Reading looks different for different people. Some people curl up with a book and binge read for hours; others might seize the five minutes between carpool or meetings to read a blog post or check out their Twitter news feed. No matter your personal preferences in what and how you read, it is vital to model reading and your love of reading with your students, staff, and families. What you model as a leader of reading will become part of the culture of reading in your school.

Share Your Love of Reading

Shortly after I graduated from college, many of my friends moved away. I was left living in a town where I didn't know many people, so when I was invited to my first book club, I eagerly accepted, read the book, and looked forward to our discussion. I hoped that the book club would be a way to meet new people and build connections in the community, but what I didn't realize was how quickly we would bond over books and the love of reading. Those relationships are some of the most powerful and intimate I've experienced.

There are many benefits to sharing your love of reading with others. In my book club, we shared new titles and encouraged reading in different genres to challenge our thinking or reading comfort zones. I looked to that group for new book recommendations or ideas, and when we discussed the books, I gained new insights from listening to the differing viewpoints. My first book club taught me that sharing the love of reading and discussing books is just as vital as the action of reading the books themselves.

When we share our reading experiences with others, our own experiences are improved. In a society that thrives on connectedness and relationships, talking about what we're reading provides meaningful and effective ways to connect. As a leader, you can cultivate a love of literacy in your school by ensuring that everyone shares their reading experiences. Here are a few ways to set the example.

A person who won't read has no advantage
over one who can't read.
—Mark Twain

Maintain a Digital Reading Log

Although there are many great tools out there for cataloging and sharing your reading journey with others, I really like GoodReads (goodreads.com). This online community allows readers to inventory their books, complete reading challenges, share their reflections, rate their selections, connect with other readers, and maintain a "to-read" list. Using GoodReads, you can easily embed a bookshelf widget onto a blog, webpage, or email signature to constantly share your reading updates. GoodReads also allows readers to find suggested books or ideas for further reading based on topics of interest or connections.

PIRATE
Leader Resource

goodreads.com

Maintaining a digital reading log also helps me set personal and professional reading goals, monitor my progress, and reflect on what I have read. And because GoodReads allows you to "friend" other readers, you can see others' lists and recommendations. I frequently look to other educators and administrators on Goodreads to find interesting titles that they have read to add to my book list. I then refer to my to-read list when selecting a new book.

Display What You Are Reading

Not all your staff, students, or parents will click through a digital reading log, so go analog. Display a simple sign sharing what you're reading outside your office. In fact, you can have all your staff do this. Imagine the power of having every teacher, support staff member, assistant, cook, and school volunteer share their current book. That kind of reading display clearly communicates a simple and powerful message that is reinforced throughout the school: *Reading is important to us, and it should be important to you!* It unifies and subtly reinforces the message that we are all learners and part of a culture of reading. When students know the adults around them are reading, they are given a strong model for lifelong reading.

The signs don't have to be elaborate. Simply print out a letter-size page with the header, "What I am Reading." Leave space for staff to write in their current book. Ask them to display it in an area outside their classroom or office door. Laminate the signs so they can be updated frequently with dry-erase markers. Alternatively, you could use sticky notes to post new book titles.

As you do walk-throughs in the building, snap pictures of current book titles on display and share them periodically in school newsletters, staff memos, and social media posts to the school community. Knowing what teachers are reading opens opportunities for meaningful conversations. There are no rules about what people can write on their "What I'm Reading" sign. It can be a children's book they are reading with their own children, a professional book, or a fictional book for personal enjoyment. The power and value of this practice comes in sharing the importance of reading.

Principal Greg Fairchild (@gjfairchild) has two posters outside his office wall to share his reading life. One displays images of the books he has recently finished learning and studying, and the other shows what books he is currently reading. This action sends a message to the staff, students, and visitors in his building that he is a lead learner.

Sharing your personal reading display offers your school community a glimpse into your life as a leader and learner. When you display what you are reading, you are laying the foundation for conversations about the books with your students, teachers, and staff. It's a simple way to open the door to meaningful dialogue about books.

Tweet It Out

Twitter is an avenue for educators to share, collaborate, and connect on any number of topics or content areas, including literacy and reading. I find many of my favorite book recommendations from other educators on Twitter who have shared a #bookshelfie, image of their current book, or stack of their to-read books.

Tweeting #booksnaps of your reflections as you read is an engaging and relevant way to share what you are reading. Tara Martin (@taramartinedu) is the creator of #booksnaps. She developed the idea of using icons, emojis, and text over images of book texts for readers to share their reflections and insights related to the text. She then encourages readers to share these #booksnaps with others on their social media.

As you acquire new books or finish the final page of an amazing book, take the time to tweet it out. Snapping a picture and posting it on social media has expanded my professional learning network (PLN) as people love to connect over the books.

Twitter also serves as a great avenue for you and your teachers and students to reach out to authors. Take reading to the next level by having students use classroom Twitter accounts to engage in reflection of books or tweet to the authors whose books they are reading. Few things are more powerful when it comes to encouraging student reading than forming a bond between them and their favorite authors. Twitter provides the perfect platform to make these connections.

Create a "Face to Face with Authors" Display

Reading a text and connecting with the message and content can impact teaching and learning. Connecting and learning directly with the author can be transformational. Through the various conferences, workshops, and events I have attended as a teacher and administrator,

I have had the chance to have face-to-face meetings with several authors and educational leaders. When I snap the selfie, it serves not only to commemorate meeting the individual but also to showcase the power of reading and connectedness to staff and students.

I post the selfie alongside a picture of the author's book cover on a wall that reads "Face to Face with Authors: Leaders are Readers!" Staff and students see this display grow as I meet some of my favorite authors. Many of the connections I have made with these authors have come on the heels of building relationships on Twitter and developing a PLN that includes industry leaders and trailblazers.

This same concept can be replicated even if you haven't had the chance to meet the authors of the books you are reading. In the school setting, we have ample access to authors. The display could include pictures of the principal or teachers posing for a picture with students who have published their writing in their classroom. Imagine the thrill a student would experience seeing their picture up on the "Face to Face with Authors" display, knowing that their teacher or principal read their work and provided feedback. Showcasing their accomplishments highlights the importance of literacy and deepens the connection and relationship for the student to the school and classroom.

Build a Professional Library

My dad is a retired police officer. Growing up, he was the toughest and strongest man I knew. In my eyes, he was made of stone and was impermeable to any emotion that would make him be perceived as weak. I always knew my dad loved me. He cheered me on at sporting events or activities. He frequently told me he loved me. I grew up in a very loving environment, but it was rare to see him crack and show any emotion.

As I prepared for high-school graduation and my first year of college, I had no idea what sacrifices my parents had to make to afford me that opportunity. I only realize now that the cost of a college education, even with scholarships and student loans, took a lot of work, extra hours, saving, and pinching pennies to make happen for me. That being said, with pride beaming from his eyes, my dad gifted me the most beautifully crafted desk set of dictionaries as a gift with a powerful message that propelled me to continue my path as a lifelong learner, reader, and lover of education.

Inside the front cover of the first volume of the dictionaries, my dad inscribed, "May these books be of good use to you in a long and happy educational career. You're a special girl, and the sky's the limit— so spread your wings and fly." When he gave me those dictionaries, he cracked, and I saw a rare glimpse of the softness and vulnerability in his heart.

Through his words and actions, my dad taught me about the power in taking risks, seizing opportunities to challenge yourself, and the value of hard work. As he hugged me and gifted that set of dictionaries, it was a symbol of the importance of learning. I've only always wanted to make him and my mom proud. Those two dictionaries sit on the bookshelf in my library as an ever-present reminder of the importance of hard work, perseverance, risk taking, sacrifice, gratitude, and learning.

When I became a teacher, and then a principal, I knew the importance of growing a library. After all, leaders are readers. Reading serves as a source of reflection, stress relief, and motivation. In books, I learn new strategies, find inspiration to try new ideas, and connect with best practices. As my professional library grows, I frequently refer to many of my books for inspiration, direction, or resources. The books in my library become springboards for faculty meeting agendas, resources for problem-solving, or sources of inspiration for a school or classroom idea or activity. Through the years, I've had to add shelves to my libraries at home and in my school office because I'm *always* reading and adding to my collection.

One of the best parts of having a strong and plentiful professional library is the ability to recommend and share books with colleagues and staff. As I finish a book, I am often inspired and seek opportunities to share new titles with staff.

So grow your professional library. Seek suggestions for your next read. Encourage others to borrow your books—and share their own. Expand your knowledge and understanding of your field through reading, collecting, and growing your own professional library.

Share What You Are Reading with Staff

It can be difficult to schedule time to get the staff together outside of faculty meetings and professional-learning community meetings. My communication with staff should emphasize lifelong learning and incorporate information to extend their own professional learning. Just as I share what I am reading with our families through our school newsletter, I also share my reading with staff. At the bottom of my weekly staff memos is a place reserved for "What I Am Currently Reading." This again models the importance I place on reading and on being consistent learners and consumers of knowledge. Sharing my reading material with staff also informs them of the books I am adding to my professional library for them to borrow or ask me about.

You can use a multimedia source to write your staff memo or family newsletter, which enables you to include links to book reviews, images of the book cover, or even video messages, or introductions from the author to share your excitement about a book. I've been using Smore Pages (smore.com) to create my staff memos and find it easy to embed links, images, and videos to showcase the book, key takeaways, links to resources, and more. When I review or finish a book by a particular author, I can use my newsletter to share concepts from the book with my staff.

An email signature is another ideal place to put your current books and demonstrate your commitment to reading to families, community members, and staff members. Place a book title, picture, or link to a GoodReads account as an opportunity to remind those you email of your commitment to reading.

Blog

My work day looks different every day; maybe you can relate. On any given day, my job might include meeting with staff to discuss an observation or evaluation, meeting with parents to discuss a concern or create a plan, working with students, and addressing any of the other myriad of items that come across my desk: answering emails, balancing building budgets, ordering instructional supplies, developing professional-development activities, hiring staff, completing state reports, monitoring lunchtime, visiting classrooms, greeting students at the door, dropping handwritten notes, recognizing positive behavior, and so much more.

Regardless of how busy I am, I make time to blog. Honestly, I was a hesitant blogger at first. I didn't feel that my words were important or valid enough to share. That being said, I understood the importance of reflection and connected learning. I also firmly believe in the connectedness of reading and writing: Readers are writers and writers are readers. So I make time to read and write. Blogging is a meaningful practice that provides me with an outlet to reflect on and share my experiences, reading, ideas, resources, and thoughts with other like-minded professionals. It is part of being a connected educator.

My blog also models reflective learning with my staff and demonstrates that I value reflection and sharing of educational practices. During a recent teacher evaluation training, our presenter focused on the key elements that make a great teacher. He stressed that excellent teachers make a point to grow professionally and share their learning and expertise with others. Why would I expect that from my staff if I am not willing to lead by example? So I make the time to blog. I share my blog posts with my staff and, in many cases, with our students' families and the greater community. When staff, students, and families read the blog, it creates a ripple effect in which books, strategies, and ideas are shared, discussed, or attempted.

When you showcase what you're reading and encourage others in your school to do the same, you demonstrate that reading is for *everyone*. Find ways to share your reading with your staff, students, larger school community, and your PLN. If you aren't already a blogger and don't know what to blog about, write about what you're reading. Remember, there are no rules about what to read—read for fun, read for learning, but, most of all, read to lead.

Reflect on Your Example as the Lead Reader

Leadership Treasure Hunt
(Find This)

Find a few books in your professional library that
you can lend to a staff member or colleague.

Navigating the Seas
(Think About This)

What books are the cornerstones of your professional library?
What about those books has made you a better educator?

Charting the Course
(Take Action)

What is a commitment you can make to showcase
and communicate what you are reading with
staff and students?

Share your thoughts and ideas!
#LeadLAP

SECTION II

SET SAIL WITH STUDENTS

*To learn to read is
to light a fire; every
syllable that
is spelled out
is a spark.*

−Victor Hugo

I've been heavily influenced by many readers in my life but none more than Regie Routman and Donalyn Miller. These two women have shaped my philosophy of reading instruction; I have been empowered by their insights into developing a love of reading in our students. As I participated in some intense professional learning centered on the beliefs of Regie Routman, one question posed during the experience was, "Does your learning environment mirror your instructional philosophy and beliefs about literacy instruction?"

Many educators say that they believe in the importance of literacy, but if we are to develop a true love for reading, the environment and school culture must support and reflect that belief. We create an environment that supports literacy by displaying (and regularly updating) signs to show what we're reading. We show that we believe reading is important when we hang library bins on the hallway walls for easy access, stock bookshelves in the cafeteria for students to access after they eat, put bookshelves in the foyer for children to access at dismissal time while they wait for their rides, or create reading nooks in the hallways so children have a quiet spot to read.

Lining the building with books in nooks, crannies, and corners specifically communicates that reading *is* important and that we value it in all areas of our lives. As educators, our goals should include a focus to "develop a culture of readers." That means giving them access to books and opportunities to read—with no strings (or test scores) attached.

Ask yourself this question: "Does your environment mirror your values and beliefs?" If your strategic plan includes a goal somewhere to create lifelong learners or avid readers, I challenge you to reflect on what practices and physical environmental characteristics you have in place to promote that. When a visitor, parent, or community member walks down the halls of your building or into a classroom, is it evident that reading and literacy are the primary focuses for you and your staff?

- Are the wall and bulletin-board displays reflecting this goal and promoting literacy?
- Are the common spaces providing access to books with no strings attached?
- Are the books available to students current and engaging?
- Do students have access to various genres and differing levels that pique their interests?
- Are there books in other areas of your school building outside your library and classrooms?
- What models of reading do students have?
- When you look around your school building, what structures do you see that support your claims or intentions?
- How can you shift from reading for a grade to reading for entertainment?

Developing a culture of readers requires intense focus on providing a literacy-rich and immersive environment for students and staff. This can be done by setting SAIL with four distinct elements of a PIRATE leader-reading environment:

Student Choice

Ample Access

Independent Reading Time

Literature-Rich Learning Environment

In this section, we'll look each of these elements and how you can use them to create an environment that supports a culture of reading and a love for literacy.

STUDENT CHOICE

Enthusiasm is the often the
missing element to engagement.
—Lead Like a PIRATE

Think of the last time you went to a bookstore or library to select a new book. You most likely had an idea of the type of book or genre you were interested in reading. You likely went to an aisle for a specific book on your reading list or to an area to peruse books on a topic or genre of interest. You likely used your prior knowledge about an author, title, or a recommendation to find a book to select out of the vast number of choices. If you were truly just browsing for a new book, perhaps you chose a title based on its cover, summary, or by flipping casually through its pages to preview it. If this is how we choose a book, why is it often so different for our students?

I sat in my office one afternoon when a group of fifth-grade girls excitedly charged into my office with the plan of launching a book club in their grade level. The group of girls included students that possessed various characteristics that were vastly different from each other. Among the girls was a student who received special education services; one who received gifted-and-talented services; one with social, emotional, and behavioral challenges; and one who had recently transferred to our school from a bilingual program in Europe. One characteristic unified the group. All the girls were set on reading and sharing *The Land of Stories* by Chris Colfer. This was not a book assigned to them in class or part of a required novel study. The book club was their plan, and the book was their choice, and both of those factors motivated them to read.

Not knowing what the result of their plan would be, I supported the idea enthusiastically and ordered their books immediately. I ordered myself a copy too. We met at lunchtime and collectively set reading goals to discuss the book. When the setting was a dungeon, I walked them to the maintenance room in the basement of the school. There was no more eerie space in the school, but it was the perfect backdrop to set the mood for the story. When a tea party was held in the forest, I transformed our office into a magical garden. When the characters went on a hunt for items and ultimately attended a ball, I mirrored those experiences in our time together.

We built an excitement for reading together that would have been squelched if I had not given their suggestion for a book club a chance. Each of the girls brought a unique perspective to our group based on their individual characteristics and experiences. I teared up when the girl who received special education services shared that reading the book at home with her mom was the highlight of her week and that it bonded them closer together. That's what reading does. I beamed with pride when the child with behavioral challenges set a goal to be more like the main character and exude compassion and empathy for others. My heart grinned when the student from a bilingual program acquired new vocabulary words and language skills by listening to her peers discuss their favorite elements of the book. I called home for the gifted child to share how proud I was of her leadership and guidance of the other students during the entire book club experience.

What this experience reinforced was that students of all reading levels and behavioral needs are capable of being readers when they are given a choice and allowed to discuss books that interest them. Students engage with books in different ways and are motivated through choice. They can perform at high levels when engaged and engulfed in the power of a story that pulls them in. As we wrapped up our final session of the book, the girls collectively and eagerly asked if we could order the second book and continue our time together. The answer was, of course, "*Yes!*"

We need to give up control over choosing books for our students and allow them the ownership and accountability to choose books that are appropriate and meaningful to them. We need to give up control that reading instruction needs to be a scripted or scheduled part of the day. Opportunities for reading can occur at any point in the school day. Even more, creating a true culture of readers means that readers extend reading past their school day. This does not mean that students might not need guidance and direction to find a book that's the right fit at their reading level, but it does mean that students should be able to choose books that speak to them. When student choice is combined with ample

PIRATE Leader Resource

A great resource to provide students in exploring books and determining book selections is whatshouldireadnext.com. This site allows students to review book suggestions based on their previous preferences and gives them freedom over their book choices.

access to reading material, teachers can begin to create *readers* rather than students who simply comply with the task of reading.

Student choice also means keeping current and relevant titles in classroom and school libraries and providing students with recommendations and choices that interest them as readers. Teachers and leaders must ensure that students have a balanced choice of texts that include classic literature as well as current books that are of high interest. We can do this by being active readers of children's literature and young adult titles.

If you are going to get anywhere in life
you have to read a lot of books.
—Roald Dahl

Reflect on Student Choice

Leadership Treasure Hunt
(Find This)

Ask your students and teachers what they are
interested in reading. Do you have books in your
school and classroom libraries on those topics?

Navigating the Seas
(Think About This)

In what ways do students in your school or classroom
have a choice or voice in their reading selections?

Charting the Course
(Take Action)

Read at least one new, popular book this month that
would be appropriate for or interesting to the students
in your school. Share it with a colleague or student.

Share your thoughts and ideas!
#LeadLAP

AMPLE ACCESS

A capacity, and taste for reading, gives access to
whatever has already been discovered by others.
—Abraham Lincoln

I was providing a tour to a new family one day when they noticed that books were everywhere. A bathtub filled with books sits in the main hallway, and bookshelves line the foyer. We display books outside the bathrooms and on colorful bookshelves strategically placed throughout the school hallways. Most importantly, no clipboards or sign-out sheets account for the books. When the child on the tour asked me what the books in the hallway were for, my answer was simply, "To read." I went on to explain that we keep books available for students to access any time they needed or wanted a book. Questions continued about how they check them out, how we hold students accountable for returning them, and who managed the logistics. My simple reply was (and continues to be), "Our school provides students ample access to books with no strings attached."

Providing ample access to books is an essential component in developing a culture of readers. It ensures that students have frequent opportunities to engage with books throughout the school day. It also allows students with limited access to books outside the classroom to have easy access to books they can take home. There are no strings attached, just books available for students when and where they need them.

Bathtub of Books

You may be wondering if "bathtub of books" is code for something. Nope, it's a literal bathtub filled with books instead of bubbles. As our building-leadership team was discussing how we could provide students access to books in the hallways in fun and unique ways, a staff member chimed in saying that she had a claw-foot tub already painted in our school colors in her garage that she was looking to get rid of. She was more than happy to donate the tub, and we were thrilled to have an eye-catching way to promote reading. It was fate.

Initially, the idea was to put the tub in a nook in our hallway; students could climb in the tub and read in a cozy spot. After a semester or so of struggling through the logistics of supervision of the bathtub and how to schedule its use, we looked at alternative uses that would be more effective and support the mission of developing a culture of readers.

We slowly started adding donated books to the bathtub, and students slowly started stopping by to rummage through the titles before and after school and throughout the day. As time went on, the bathtub filled with books donated to our school by families and community members. Today, students regularly rifle through the tub to look for new titles and take books home. The most important aspect of this tub is that students have access to books with no strings attached. They are encouraged to take books home. They can keep them or bring them back at their leisure. Students are also aware that this is a place to donate books that they no longer want or need.

The bathtub isn't the important aspect to focus on here. What's most important about our "bathtub library" is that students have a fun and engaging location to search for and find books. They can choose what to read, and they are free to take the books home without any stipulations on when or if to return it. Your free-access library could be a bathtub, but it could also be a phone booth, bookshelf, boat, pool, or any other vessel. What's important is to give students open access to books with no strings attached.

Reading Emergency Shelves

Let's think about a traditional school library and how the system works. A student goes in, finds a book they are interested in, and checks it out. The child either reads through it quickly and has to wait until the next "library day" to choose a new book, or they don't finish it and return it anyway because it is their "library day." If they lose it, they are fined and cannot check out another book until it is paid for or returned.

Now I realize that we need systems and procedures for running libraries in an effort to maintain inventory and develop responsibility and accountability in our students. But I also know that we need to provide access to books if we want to encourage readers and ensure our environment mirrors our values and beliefs when it comes to reading and literacy. Students should have enough access to books that every day has the potential to be "library day."

I learned from Donalyn Miller that readers should always have a book with them in the event of a "reading emergency." These are the times in our day where we might have a spare moment to read. In a school setting, it could be the transition to a class, waiting in line for picture day, or after finishing a task or test. Miller's idea prompted the establishment of "Reading Emergency Bookshelves" in our school. These bookshelves are strategically placed throughout the building in areas where students and visitors can access easily them. The shelves are filled with books that have been donated to our school over time and include a variety of reading levels, genres, and topics. There is no inventory system, no expectation to return the books—just an open invitation to take a book and read it when you need it.

The placement of the bookshelves can and should be balanced across the layout of the school, but here are a few areas where they are most frequently used:

- The entrance of the building where students can access them at the start of their day
- The main foyer or area where students wait for transportation at dismissal time
- The lunchroom
- Above water fountains
- In the main office where visitors or students wait
- Outside a counselor's office
- Outside restrooms for when students might wait for others to exit.

Books are the perfect entertainment: no commercials, no batteries, hours of enjoyment for each dollar spent. What I wonder is why everyone doesn't carry around a book for those inevitable dead spots in life.
—Stephen King

Do the shelves get a little disheveled? Yes. Do they need some attention on occasion? Yes. A great solution to this, without adding staff time, is to organize a student group dedicated to maintaining the shelves. It is an opportunity to develop student leadership and promote literacy at the same time. Win-win!

Provide Access to Books 24/7 with Little Free Libraries

I am always on the lookout to develop or implement additional ways to embed elements in my school and community that promote a love of reading and literacy. As I was celebrating a college football victory in Iowa City, Iowa, I came across a Little Free Library (littlefreelibrary.org) nestled between two trees on a busy corner at an intersection, and many fans cloaked in black and gold were passing by. On most days, it is a busy but pedestrian-friendly thoroughfare. With a park bench to the side and a quaint cobblestone path leading to it, I was instantly drawn to the structure with its clear window revealing a variety of books. A placard that read "Little Free Library" explained that the contents were maintained to provide anyone passing by with a free book. It also encouraged those who could to donate books for others to enjoy. Thus, my love for the Little Free Libraries began.

Little Free Libraries can and have been placed anywhere. In fact, there are more than fifty thousand Little Free Libraries around the world that provide access to books 24/7 to children and adults. Since that first Little Free Library encounter, I have seen them in parks, community centers, local neighborhoods, and schools.

We've even established one on our school property. The not-for-profit agency that created the concept makes it easy. You can order structures directly from them or download plans to build one yourself. Within a few weeks of ordering, we had our structure, painted it, and were ready for the grand opening. With a press release, red ribbon, and ceremonial scissors borrowed from our local chamber of commerce, we held a ribbon-cutting ceremony followed by an opportunity for all of our staff and students to read outside for a period of time to celebrate our new Little Free Library.

The Little Free Library is close to the school entrance and can be accessed by students as they enter or leave the building, by staff and visitors throughout the day, and by community members at all hours. Although it's easy enough to check and stock it regularly, it is amazing to see how frequently donations are made. Visitors help keep it tidy and post about it on social media.

We had such success with our first Little Free Library, we placed one on our playground. Our playground is accessible to the community after hours, as is the Little Free Library. But the intent in placing it on the playground was to provide students who wanted to spend their recreational and play time engaged in a book the option to do so. At various points in the year, students might choose to read, play on the equipment, or participate in any other recess activity of their choice. I love to see our students immersing themselves in reading, sharing books with friends, or having conversations about reading. The Little Free Library is open and available all day, every day. When school is not in session on weekends and breaks, our students and community still have access to books. The key is providing the option and making books available and easily accessible—again, with no strings attached.

PIRATE Leader Resource

Learn more about this movement
and put your school on the map by
installing your own Little Free Library.
Visit littlefreelibrary.org to find out how.

Treasure from the Trenches
Stock Them Up for Summer

Jay Billy believes that literacy is an equalizer. Realizing that his students don't always have access to books during the summer months, he went on a mission to promote summer reading. Jay and his dedicated staff members completed interest inventories and used grant funding and support from their parent-teacher organization (PTO) to ensure all students received twelve books—at their reading level and matched to their interests—for the summer. Their efforts sent a clear message to students and families that *we are readers all the time!*

Schools share a common goal to develop and cultivate the best learning environments for students so that they can become the best versions of themselves. Despite where you may work and lead, we all have students who come from varied backgrounds and have differing experiences with and exposure to books. Some of our students come from homes where books are priorities, and their shelves are laden with the newest titles. These children might frequent the library or bookstore because books are an everyday part of their lives. Other students come from homes where books are not easily found, and the shelves are bare. In some homes, screen time and technology devices trump the power of a quality book and the bond of a child reading with their parent. To develop a culture of reading, we need to give our students reading options—letting them choose what to read—and make sure they have ample access to books throughout the year.

—Jay Billy (@jaybill2), principal and author of *Lead with Culture*

Reflect on Ensuring Access to Books

Leadership Treasure Hunt
(Find This)

In what ways do you promote and provide access to books 24/7 to students?

Navigating the Seas
(Think About This)

In what ways do you ensure that students have ample access to high-quality books?

Charting the Course
(Take Action)

Find nooks and crannies (or bathtubs or other unique storage options) waiting to be filled with books for your students. Ask your school community for donations of quality, used books.

Share your thoughts and ideas!
#LeadLAP

INDEPENDENT READING TIME

*Intentional time and focus devoted to the right things
are what will ultimately propel you forward.*
—Lead Like a PIRATE

My first teaching job was in a seventh-grade, self-contained special education classroom. I firmly believe that everyone has career-defining moments and memories from their first year of teaching. I know I had mine. As a first-year teacher, I was convinced I was going to make waves in education and make an immediate impact on the learners in my classroom. I loved teaching. I loved kids. I loved learning. So imagine how disillusioning it was to have students who were not only several grade levels below where they should have been in reading but who also had a genuine distaste for school that began the moment they stepped foot in kindergarten due to their academic difficulties and challenges.

I conducted the mandatory scripted lessons from our prescribed curriculum each day, but my students and I both struggled with the monotony of the required curriculum materials. I knew that my students weren't inspired to be readers. I wasn't inspired as their teacher. Not many high-interest, low-readability books were available to us. Understandably, they didn't want to read the books at their instructional or independent reading level because the content was either boring or "babyish" to them.

Despite a limited classroom library common to new teachers, I focused on begging and borrowing new and used books to build the library. I knew early in my career that the power of reading came from connecting with books, characters, and authors—which only comes through time spent reading. I knew that if I grew my library and continued to recommend books, my students could grow to love reading.

Looking back on that year, I would have changed so much, but I learned so much as well. One of the biggest lessons I learned that year came from a twelve-year-old named Anthony as he sat in my new but sparse classroom library and thumbed through some of the books on CD that I had recently inherited. He was completely capable of comprehending text at grade level but struggled so much with decoding and fluency that reading an engaging text felt laborious and not worth the challenge. He came across a title with a dragon on the front cover that pulled him in. He asked to listen to the book on CD with the novel in front of him. The book, *Eragon*, was significantly higher than his independent reading level, but he was able to follow along by listening to the CD. The story grabbed his attention, and he became enamored with the story shortly into the book. Every day, he raced to the reading corner to hear more of the tale. When he finished that book and eagerly asked me for the second book in the series, I didn't care that I was on a first-year teacher's salary and really couldn't afford the thirty dollars for a CD and book. I bought it anyhow. It was the best money I spent. In the following weeks, he devoured the next few books in the series and learned of similar series that he followed up with. It might have been by chance, but he left my classroom a reader.

The canned curriculum didn't make Anthony a reader. A powerful story did that just like I had experienced as a fourth-grade student. Those stories gave him a glimpse into the world of books, and he found a mode that allowed him to access this wonder despite his disability. But Anthony's love of reading would never have developed had it not been for independent reading time. Yes, as his teacher, I worked with him to build the foundational skills he needed so that he could more effectively decode and fluently read words. But our biggest success that year was improving his reading comprehension and vocabulary, which happened because he was finally accessing books that engaged him and made him *want* to read. Independent reading time—and the freedom to choose a book he was interested in—were central to this success.

Find Time for Independent Reading

Students need independent reading time, and they need to be explicitly taught and reminded how to seize time during the day to develop strong reading habits. Think of all the transition times during the day that could be an opportunity to read:

- Bathroom breaks
- Picture day
- Waiting to go into art or music class
- Finishing a test early
- End-of-day dismissal
- Bus rides to and from school
- Field trip transportation

Each of those times, and so many more, are appropriate opportunities to engage students in the reading process. Teachers need to also understand and preserve independent reading time within their block of reading instruction. Reading independently develops comprehension, fluency, vocabulary, and stamina for reading. Readers will grow with increased independent reading time. Students need support and instruction on how to identify and seize these opportunities to read.

I have always imagined that paradise will be a kind of library.
—Jorge Luis Borges

Reflect on Independent Reading Opportunities

Leadership Treasure Hunt
(Find This)

How much time, if any, do your teachers currently devote
to independent reading time in their classes?

Navigating the Seas
(Think About This)

How do you protect independent reading time in your school
or classroom? In what ways could you seize additional
reading minutes throughout the school day?

Charting the Course
(Take Action)

Promote independent reading time and hold an
all-school reading experience where all staff
and students engage in independent reading.

Share your thoughts and ideas!
#LeadLAP

LEARNING ENVIRONMENT

People are less likely to tear down
systems they help to build.
—Lead Like a PIRATE

icture your favorite location to read. For me, it is either curled up on my couch on a cold rainy day with a blanket, cup of coffee, and the fireplace crackling in the background or while reclining in a lounge chair at a tropical vacation spot. On a more regular basis, I like to read while sitting on my bed or in a comfy chair. None of those ideal locations have anything to do with a hard desk or industrial office chair, which are frequently the settings for reading in a traditional classroom.

The physical learning environment has a lot to do with what and how we communicate our vision and mission for reading. If we are striving to develop lifelong learners with a focus on developing a culture of readers, then our physical learning spaces need to adapt to meet that goal; learning spaces need to be comfortable and collaborative.

Creating seating options for students to access during independent reading places value on the reading and on the student's level of comfort. Comfortable and collaborative reading areas could include the following:

- Couches
- Comfortable chairs
- Cushions and pillows
- Scoop chairs or rockers
- Yoga mats
- Ball seats
- Tents
- Book nooks
- Lawn chairs
- Wading pools

Promote Flexible Seating Across the School Environment

Comfortable and collaborative learning spaces extend outside the classroom. To truly envelop a school culture in reading, these spaces can and should be found in hallways, nooks, and common spaces. Imagine how collaborative learning spaces and reading nooks in these common areas can promote your mission and vision related to reading. Look around your school and ask these questions:

- Can we use our current areas in ways that promote comfortable reading spaces?
- Are there areas in the building that we can infuse with comfortable seating that would promote reading in our students?
- Do we make seating available near our books to promote sporadic and spontaneous acts of reading?
- Do we have spaces available outside that promote literacy and reading?
- Where could you add beanbags, comfortable chairs, or alternative seating to enhance the common spaces in your school?

#BookShelfie Station

I was picking up a new dress at a local boutique when I spotted a frame hanging on the wall with the hashtag of the boutique. It was there for patrons to snap a selfie after they purchased a new outfit or accessories. My mind is always looking for creative ways to incorporate ideas into the school setting, and I immediately thought of a #bookshelfie station. I purchased a large blue frame from a local thrift store and had a simple decal made at a printing shop. We then found the perfect spot in the hallway for the #bookshelfie station. Students stop and take selfies with the books they are reading and then share them with friends, teachers, and staff. I also encourage staff members to take their #bookshelfies (posing with their favorite books, of course), and post them on social media accounts and in their classrooms. It's a simple strategy that reinforces a love of reading and learning.

Teddy Time: Using Facility Dogs in the Learning Environment

When I was a kindergarten student, my principal had an English sheepdog, Chewie, that lazily laid outside her office. It was her personal pet that she brought to work each day. Chewie was beloved by the staff and students and made his way into the school composite picture and yearbook.

If a child was sick, the dog would nuzzle up to them and distract them until a parent arrived. If a visitor came to the office, the dog's sweet disposition instantly brought a smile. Chewie would "read" with students in the hallway. He was an important element of the school climate and culture.

All these years later, I still have vivid memories of that dog. So when I became a special education teacher, the research that supports service dogs in education intrigued me for many reasons. My memories of Chewie made the benefits of placing service dogs with students seem obvious.

When I became principal, I had an eager volunteer, a trusted mainstay in the building with a passion for two things: working with kids and training service dogs. When she suggested she bring in her dogs a day or two a week, I enthusiastically agreed. We started with a small group of struggling students whom she met with one-on-one. The students and the volunteer read books together with the dog nestled between them.

After one visit to our school, she planted a seed about the benefits of having a full-time facility dog. Facility dogs are expertly trained dogs who partner with facilitators in professional environments. The dogs can perform more than forty commands, all tailored to the environment and designed to motivate and inspire their clients. The organization had placed a few in specialized environments—prisons, special education centers, and hospitals—and witnessed the immediate rewards and benefits. She thought our school would be a great fit for a facility dog and shared with me the long list of benefits. Facility dogs can . . .

- Help reduce symptoms of stress, anxiety, and depression
- Help process grief and loss
- Help students open up about issues impacting them emotionally/academically
- Help students with communication difficulties improve social skills
- Help student with sensory integration needs to improve language production and social interaction
- Help reluctant readers improve fluency
- Help make the office a more welcoming and inviting place
- Help increase overall staff and student morale and positive connection to school

A trained and certified facility dog can complete many tasks and be utilized to support academics, social and behavioral needs, and literacy in many ways.

Individual Students

The dog can assist students who demonstrate the following symptoms/behaviors:

- Anxiety/panic attacks
- Depression
- Grief/loss
- Stress
- Limited socialization with peers
- Limited motivation to attend school

Classrooms/Groups

The dog's presence in various groups and classrooms can also be helpful in a number of ways:

- Classroom visits to build positive relationships
- Lower tension and stress
- Support individuals in distress
- Provide sensory support for students with sensory integration needs
- Assist in reading fluency activities for struggling/ reluctant readers

Facility dogs can also be part of the school crisis team to lessen trauma of critical incident/event for students, teachers, and staff. Knowing the benefits of a facility dog, I took a risk and navigated the necessary channels and completed the required research to apply for one in my school. Within a year of the application and continued visits by our dedicated volunteer, a standard poodle named Teddy Royal was born. For fifteen months, Teddy underwent intense service-dog training. He was placed in our school with our school secretary as his handler.

Teddy is just as much a part of our school culture now as Chewie was for me as a kindergarten student. Teddy reads with individual and small groups of students, easing their fear and anxiety related to their abilities and focusing on growing a love of reading. Teddy is used as a reward for positive behavior and meeting reading goals. Students can opt to schedule time to read with Teddy or have him visit their classrooms. Sometimes, creating a culture to support reading means looking at alternatives and creative opportunities that will make meaningful, safe, and memorable experiences for our students. When I see a student reading with Teddy, my heart knows that the student will remember him thirty years from now just as I remember Chewie. Reading is just as much about what is in the environment to support the development of readers as it is about the text. That means making sure you have comfortable seating, fun ways to share their reading, and maybe even the opportunity to snuggle with a furry friend like Teddy for support.

Reflect on Your School's Learning Environment

Leadership Treasure Hunt
(Find This)

Where is the most comfortable place to read in your school? What elements of that area make it comfortable? How can that feeling be replicated in other areas throughout your building?

Navigating the Seas
(Think About This)

How could you adapt the learning environment in your school and classroom to create comfortable and inviting reading nooks or areas?

Charting the Course
(Take Action)

Set up your own #bookshelfie station to encourage students and staff members to share their reading.

Share your thoughts and ideas!
#LeadLAP

SECTION III

READ.
CONNECT.
REPEAT.

*There's so much
more to a book
than just reading.*

—Maurice Sendak

Think about your favorite songs. Do certain songs jog memories? I am sure the answer is yes. The same is true with books. I can remember the basal reader from first grade when I learned to read for the first time. I felt success and pride at that point. I can remember reading *How to Eat Fried Worms* in fourth grade and a boy in my class taking on the challenge himself. I felt disgusted and shocked while reading that book. I remember reading *Pinballs* in fifth grade and specifically recall the deep sadness I felt for the children in that story and how truly lucky and blessed I was.

Books have the power to evoke so many emotions, and I have connected with hundreds of books over my lifetime in an emotionally charged way. In many cases, I can remember the sights and sounds around me when I read those books. Just like when I hear my favorite song, when I read my favorite books, I am brought back to those moments.

Add to those powerful books an educator who builds relationships and makes reading an engaging experience for students. When that occurs, the experience is truly amplified. Like the time my fourth-grade teacher ate lunch with me and a small group of friends to discuss a favorite book we had chosen. I felt valued. Or that time a high school English teacher gifted me a book from her classroom library because I had loved the first book in the series so much. I felt heard and invigorated. Or that time I watched a third-grade teacher, Natalie Lanser, spend her own funds to purchase additional books in a series because one of her challenging students was devouring them. I felt inspired and proud.

Books by themselves have the power to forge deep and impactful connections. Books paired with meaningful relationships between students and teachers can propel a culture of reading forward. Teachers and administrators can deepen a love of reading by connecting with kids over books and literacy.

BUILD RELATIONSHIPS
WITH BOOKS

Everyone wins when highly effective
leaders bring their passion to work.
—Lead Like a PIRATE

Ellie came bounding into the office with a smile on her face, ready to take her mid-afternoon medication. She was always racing around at a mile a minute to get from one thing to the next, and I am sure her mind raced just as quickly. Before I could get a word out, she started to tell me all about a book she was reading. She went through the storyline beautifully and articulated it better than many adults I knew. You could tell she loved it. As she became even more excited while telling me about various parts of the book, her rate of speech increased, and her hands flapped wildly. She was on a roll. Jumping up and down, she told me that she couldn't wait to tell me what happened next. For several minutes, I saw this fifth grader's excitement build as she shared her reading experience with me. When I told her it was one of my favorite books and that I knew what happened next, she stopped in her tracks. A look of awe spread across her face and she said, "You've read it? Don't tell me the end!"

For the next three days, Ellie gave me daily updates about her progress in the book. Each day, her excitement and enthusiasm grew as she sought me out throughout the day to let me know at which juncture of the book she was. It became an immediate connection for us. As principal and her student, we talked daily about a book that had a significant impact on both of us. When she reached the end of the book and came to talk to me about it, she gave me the biggest hug and said, "I just loved that book and loved that we could talk about it!" Knowing that she was about to finish the book, I was ready. I handed her another book—one I knew she would love because I now knew her as a reader and more deeply as a student. She took it eagerly with a grin and bounded out of my office as quickly and happily as she had pranced in.

Books have the power to start conversations and build relationships, and we have the responsibility to cultivate those relationships and build rapport with our students.

It Starts the Moment They Walk into the Building

Kindergarten students might not be able to read yet, but they (and their parents) do have a lot of emotions about beginning a new school year. Books are a perfect opportunity to introduce them to their new school and to promote literacy. Consider adopting a few of the following ideas to showcase the importance of reading during kindergarten registration or orientation events.

Welcome-to-Kindergarten Books

Welcome new families and students with a book showcasing the various areas of the school and introducing them to staff. Have them ready for any new family that walks in the door and share it online. The books can be as simple or elaborate as you'd like them to be. You can create them simply by using Google Docs or Google Slides. Print them in color and staple or bind them. Not only will this book allow new students to showcase their new school to family and friends at home, it will also be the first time (but not the last) they bring home a book from school. It's a subtle but strategic opportunity to embed and promote literacy right off the bat.

Each page features a different area of the school with pictures and what to expect in that area. Walk them through each key part of the facility:

- Front of the school
- Office with pictures of administration and support staff
- Cafeteria with pictures of the lunch line, tables, food tray, and kitchen staff
- Media or technology lab with pictures of the devices and sample projects
- Library with a message about how frequently they will visit, what they will do there, and pictures of the space
- Classrooms
- Gymnasiums
- Auditoriums
- Hallways

Go further and offer them a water bottle with a logo or a T-shirt as a welcome gift. Smile when you see them wear it on their first day of school. After all, you are branding a culture of readers but also branding your school as a whole.

The Night Before Kindergarten Books

Our kindergarten orientation night includes a scavenger hunt in which kindergarten students and their families take a map of the school around to locate various key features that include their classroom, cafeteria, school bus, gymnasium, and the school library. It is the perfect opportunity to provide them with a keepsake and add a book to their personal libraries. As part of their self-guided tour, they locate the library where a basket of *The Night Before Kindergarten* books are waiting for them. This book by Natasha Wing shares the experience of a child preparing for kindergarten and provides examples of what students might encounter when they attend school for the first time. They are directed to sit and enjoy reading the book with their families as part of the evening. They then get to take a copy of the book home with them. Inside the book is a message from me welcoming them to our school and reiterating the importance of reading. I love knowing that students will get to take a copy home to read with their families, ease their anxiety of coming to kindergarten, and add to their home libraries.

Morning Arrival

I love morning drop off. Each morning is an opportunity to greet students and start off their day at school on a positive note despite what might have transpired at home or on the ride to school. It is an opportunity to share a simple smile, give a high five, ask for a fist bump, or help a student out of a car.

This is also the perfect time to build connections with readers and reinforce the importance of books and literacy. Think of the powerful connections you can make with kids by greeting them at the door each morning. Take it a step further and ask them about the books they are reading:

- Follow up with a student about their progress in a book
- Recommend a new book based on your knowledge of the student
- Dress up as a book character and play a mini-guessing game for students to determine the character
- Surprise a child with a book selected just for them
- Encourage continued reading of a book that has been started, but progress has been slow
- Make connections to favorite characters or plotlines
- Share current events that connect to a student's favorite book

Keep Them Reading All Summer

Summer time is the perfect time to establish a few reading events to bring students into the school building to build connections over books. Principals and staff can easily create opportunities to gather students on campus and develop a culture of readers. The frequency and theme of these events is completely up to those hosting them. The important thing is that you start. The first summer I did these types of events, I started small. I chose two dates on my summer calendar and communicated my plans to families and students.

Popsicles with the Principal

This was my first event. Students came to school, and we read three picture books with a summer theme. I contacted the local fire department to have a fire truck available for a demonstration as well. We ended the event with playtime on the playground. Between the stories, popsicles, fire truck, and playtime, we had great fun. Students made summer time connections with one another and with staff.

Doughnuts and Pajamas Story Time

A breakfast-themed event was an opportunity for students to come to school and enjoy school-colored doughnuts in their pajamas to hear two of my favorite empathy-and-kindness-building stories: *The Jelly Donut Difference* by Maria Dismondy and *The Juice Box Bully* by Bob Sornson and Maria Dismondy. We provided a simple dough-nut-themed craft and encouraged the students to play on the play-ground. The cost to provide doughnuts was minimal, but they were appreciated by the students and families who attended.

Reading Campout

Drawing students into the school building during the summer can be as simple as asking them to bring in a book and sit outside and read with staff. A reading campout is a free event that encourages independent reading as well as reading out loud. It is also a perfect opportunity to open the building to allow students access to the free books that are available.

Pop-Up Events

When I am working in the summer, it is quiet. I love being able to accomplish so much to close out the previous year and plan for the next school year, but I miss the daily interactions with staff and stu-dents. Within those quiet moments, a pop-up event occurred to me. The idea is often used with home businesses in which individuals will hold a pop-up event at a different location to sell their merchandise with little advance warning or promotion. The same concept can apply with students and reading.

You don't need much planning or notice for a pop-up event. Early in the week, send notices to families that you are planning a reading pop-up event. Spontaneously invite them in to read for a short period of time. As students come, simply read and enjoy the time to build relationships and get to know your students as readers. This doesn't have to take place at school. Think of other locations in your community that would support this idea and meet the kids there!

- Neighborhood park
- Library
- Community center
- Coffee or ice cream store
- Day care
- Nature center

Read with Them

Reading can and should be a relationship-building process that educators can use to strengthen rapport with students. When I visit classrooms, I enjoy pulling students aside and asking them what they are reading or to read to me. The one-on-one time with a young child is priceless. You gain so much insight into a child's reading preferences, academic ability, and confidence when you talk with them about reading. Often I come equipped with stickers, ribbons, or "I read with the principal" certificates to congratulate a child for their reading accomplishments.

Invite teachers to send students to the office to read with you. I enjoy it when I receive a surprise visit from a young student thrilled to finally independently read a book or a list of sight words with me for the first time. Listening patiently to a student read to me provides an opportunity to build a relationship with the student and get to know him or her as a reader. Following these reading times, I often have students ring a bell in the office, celebrating their accomplishment.

Lunchtime is another one of my favorite times to read to students. I pop in and read over the microphone in our lunchroom as students finish their meals. It doesn't require advance planning, and I can share some of my favorite stories as students listen.

Classroom read alouds also promote a culture of readers. Principals can and should volunteer to read to classrooms throughout the year. As an added bonus, the principal can allow the teacher to use that time to run a quick errand or complete a task.

Birthday Books

A book is a gift you can open again and again.
—Garrison Keillor

Reading should not be presented to children as a chore or duty. It should be offered to them as a precious gift.
—Kate DiCamillo

When I was five or six years old, my dad gave me a book for Christmas. I had received books as gifts many times before, but this time, it was different. As I opened the front cover, my dad told me the story of meeting the local authors and of having them personalize a greeting just for me inside the front cover. Their words, written especially for me, made this gift even more meaningful.

We form so many relationships with and about books and reading. When we connect over titles, topics, and genres of books, we develop a special bond with one another. That's why I love to give books as gifts. Let's be real: Pencils, erasers, crowns, or stickers can acknowledge a student on their birthday and make them feel special,

TREASURE FROM THE TRENCHES
PRINCIPAL'S MONTHLY READ
ALOUDS AND ACTIVITIES

The idea for starting the Principal's Monthly Read Alouds and Activities came from wanting to connect with students more, getting in classes to read more, teaching some character education lessons, and simply giving teachers the "gift of time."

Before the school year started, I reviewed all the picture book titles I wanted to read to students and created a simple table. I assigned one book to each month and connected it to a character development trait that I thought would reinforce our positive behavioral intervention support expectations. My assistant principal and I then took the idea a step further by adding in an activity to go along with each read aloud. The goal was to make the activities fun, engaging, and meaningful. Our student council then took it even further by assigning monthly spirit days to match the month's trait.

So how did we decide what classrooms to read to? I created a Google Calendar titled, "Monthly Read Alouds," and my assistant principal and I blocked out appointment slots during the month. Between the two of us, we set up enough appointment slots to read to at least ten to twelve classrooms each month.

—Jessica Gomez (@jgomezprincipal),
principal of Alice Birney School

but not too long after that token is given to them, they are discarded or lost. To build a culture of readers in your building, match your rewards, incentives, and gifts to your goals, vision, and philosophy.

A birthday bookshelf is an opportunity for students to come into the principal's office on their birthday, select a new book, and have it signed by the principal. During these interactions, the principal learns about the child's preferences in reading, can build a connection through a short conversation, and provides a copy of a book to the child. I have also used this time to take a #birthdayselfie with the students and send a picture to their family or post it on our school social media pages.

Any book that helps a child to form a habit of reading, to make reading one of his needs, is good for him.
—Maya Angelou

Logistics are simple: Students who are celebrating birthdays (or half birthdays for summer birthdays) are given a birthday bookmark with their name on it from the office. These are printed inexpensively at print shops or can be done on cardstock on your own. The bookmarks serve as a reminder for students to come to the office to claim their birthday book and also as a pass to indicate to office staff why the child is in the office. As the student receives their book, the bookmark goes in, and *voila*! If I am not in the office to sign a book, they can be left with the bookmark for me to sign, and I personally deliver them when I am available.

Funding for these books is made possible by our PTO. They use funds from our book fair revenue to purchase books in various levels, genres, topics, and interests for students. This is done twice a year to build inventory on the bookshelf and maintain current and popular titles. A birthday bookshelf could also be done at a classroom level with book order dollars.

Giving the gift of books sends a clear message that you value reading and that you are intentional about developing a culture of readers through your gifts and tokens.

Birthdays are also the perfect time to allow students to share their favorite titles. Many schools have strict treat policies to accommodate for health and medical concerns. Using books to celebrate birthdays circumvents that concern by encouraging students to celebrate a birthday or special occasion by bringing their favorite book from home or choosing one from the classroom library to have read on their special day or to read to the class. This strategy cultivates a sense of community and joy around books as they are embedded as part of a celebration.

Find ways to celebrate with books. When we use what we value as incentive, motivation, and celebration, we reinforce our priorities and goals. Celebrating with books is an embedded practice in the first-grade classroom of Jessica Wentz (@Jessica_A_Wentz). Jessica prepares a birthday tote bag every year for her class that is sent home with students on their birthdays. This tote bag includes a variety of picture books about celebrating birthdays that the child can read at home and return the following day. The tote bag always includes a special class book made by the students highlighting all the unique and special characteristics of the birthday child. It's a very personal memento of the student's birthday that celebrates them—in their own book.

Don't leave out your staff. Celebrate staff birthdays with a professional learning birthday bookshelf. Include the most current and compelling titles in addition to classic professional reads and allow teachers to choose their own gift. This differentiates their professional learning and supports the growth of their own professional libraries.

Give the Literal Gift of Reading

It never fails. Teacher appreciation week comes around and I rack my brain or thumb through gift catalogs to find the perfect gift to express my appreciation for the hard-working teachers in my building. I want something that shows how much I value their work but that is also practical and meaningful. After cycling through this same internal struggle each year, I have always come back to the same solution: books!

I have made it a habit to gift my staff books for teacher appreciation week. Books have always been my go-to gifts because they support professional growth and learning and our school mission and values. Books also allow me to express my appreciation through the message of the book itself.

Gifting books has multiple advantages and benefits. Gifting books will support the development of staff professional libraries. The books can be used as a larger book study or staff learning goal. Books can support and cultivate a positive culture when selected for their connection to school vision and mission.

One of the first books I gifted to staff was *The Book Whisperer* by Donalyn Miller. As staff members read the book independently, the conversations, ideas, and excitement grew and spread throughout our school. We discussed elements of the book both informally and in staff meetings, and more members of the staff read the book and began altering their philosophy and approach to reading instruction and the development of a culture of readers. Another year, I gave each staff member a copy of the inspirational book, *Kid President's Guide to Being Awesome*. I also included a personalized inscription in the front cover for each staff member, celebrating their individual gifts and talents and sharing my appreciation for their dedication and contributions to our school.

When we welcome new staff to our team, current staff sign a book that is then gifted to the new staff. The written messages convey a sense of community and family and serve as a memento and keepsake for their first year in our school family.

Once a book has been gifted, it is important to communicate and embed elements and concepts of the book within conversations with staff to keep the momentum and excitement about the book going. That can be done through weekly updates in staff memos, revisiting them during faculty meetings, or arranging author calls.

I have never regretted the money spent on books gifted to my staff. Gifting books allows me to encourage lifelong reading and learning, share my love of reading, and demonstrate the value I place on my staff and their growth.

Authors Call Teachers for Teacher Appreciation Week

One year, for Teacher Appreciation Week, I chose to gift the book *Kids Deserve It!* by Todd Nesloney and Adam Welcome. A key component to the *Kids Deserve It!* message is to "pick up the phone and call." I had an idea to apply that philosophy to teachers in a way that would make the week extra special. I reached out to my connections on Twitter and within my PLN for help, and each person I reached out to was completely supportive.

In short, I asked some of my teachers' educational heroes to make positive calls to thank them for their amazing work as educators. The "heroes" varied based on staff members and their individual interests, but they included authors and national speakers—and my staff was ecstatic! The feedback was phenomenal. Many received positive phone calls from authors of the books we have read as a staff, which strengthened the connection between the teachers and the books they had read, studied, and implemented in their classrooms. I

71

would imagine that the individuals who called my staff were equally as energized to be able to bring joy and excitement to the educators they called.

The possibilities here are endless. With the power of a PLN, authors of children's books, local or state government officials, and educational leaders could all be tapped into to make these positive calls to your staff.

Spread the Love of Reading

You can spread the love of reading throughout the year, but holidays provide an avenue to make celebrating reading even more special and intentional. For example, during the week of Valentine's Day, leave a basket of books in a common teacher work area with Valentine's Day cards. Invite teachers and staff to share a book from the basket and a personal note with a colleague or student. By making books available for this purpose, you create a culture where sharing books becomes common and supported.

Send Book-a-Grams

Picture books resonate with me on a variety of levels, and I know that, regardless of the age level or profession, a picture book out there can elaborate on a particular concept, spark a conversation, or share an inspirational message. You can spread a love of reading by sending books via mail to other educators, classrooms, or schools in your region or with whom you have connected. Think of the power in receiving an envelope with a fun book and personalized note from a colleague or connection. An important part of building a culture of readers is spreading joy and brightening the day of a fellow educator, and there's no better way to do that than sharing your love of books and reading.

Be a Mobile Lead Reader

Early in my career, I would make attempts to get out into classrooms and in the hallways but continuously felt pulled back to the office to keep up with emails, write evaluations, finish reports, and take care of other management-related tasks. It never failed that I would be down the hall or in a classroom and need my computer or want to write a note, read a book, or celebrate a student, but not have any supplies. I quickly determined that I would be better served if the necessities from my office were portable and could come with me. As a solution to that need, I created the Port-a-Principal.

The Port-a-Principal foundation is an old AV cart that was on its way to the dumpster. I spray painted it in our school color, royal blue (of course). With a couple of additions, it is now a mobile office that allows me to stay connected to email and the school secretary while being visible in the hallways and classrooms. It is stocked with stickers, sticky notes, and note cards so that I can leave notes of encouragement to staff and students, provide feedback on their work, and support their teaching and learning.

There is no such thing as a child who hates to read; there are only children who have not found the right book.
—Frank Serafini

As a model reader, it is also stocked with picture books and bookmarks that I can readily have available to recognize a student who is reading or to gift a book to a student. I keep many of my favorite read alouds on my cart for scheduled and impromptu read alouds in classrooms and with kids.

73

With all the necessities of my office, I can observe lessons, read, and engage with students and still respond to emails or situations that need my attention in the office.

Read with kids. Read to kids. Read around kids. Have books everywhere. Reading connects with kids when you don't even know it will. You never know what's going to hook them and spark that lifetime reading love!

Treasure from the Trenches

Reading is funny. It clicks for some kids but not for others. I was one of those kids it didn't click for. The frustrating part was that my dad was a teacher for thirty-eight years, and I virtually grew up in his classroom. When I read at home, it was always out loud, which frustrated my older brother to no end, but at least I was reading!

Then, in third grade, I discovered Roald Dahl, and reading clicked. When I became a principal, reading with classes was a top priority. It started with a few books my first year and then morphed into reading one book each month to every class on campus. I'd then donate that book to our library, which was always a hot checkout after I finished my rounds.

The real kicker came in year two of my principalship when, on the Monday after our school auction, the student whose family had purchased the Principal-for-a-Day opportunity (a child who was often in my office for not-so-good reasons) ran up to me before school, beyond excited to plan our activities. Number one on the list: He wanted to read his favorite picture book to every class at school. Turns out, he used to loathe reading until I started coming in monthly to read. He had begged his parents to purchase Principal for the Day so that he could now read to everyone at school. This was the ultimate case of paying it forward—from my dad, to me, and now to this former reluctant reader. I couldn't be happier.

—Adam Welcome (@awelcome),
principal and coauthor of *Kids Deserve It!*

Chapter Reflection Questions

Leadership Treasure Hunt
(Find This)

What book(s) could you gift your students or staff members?

Navigating the Seas
(Think About This)

How can you take a celebration that you currently
do in your classroom or school and add an
element of reading or literacy to it?

Charting the Course
(Take Action)

Challenge yourself to connect with a child about what
they're reading each day this week. What insights did
you gain from discussing reading with them?

Share your thoughts and ideas!
#LeadLAP

Treasure the Risks and Rewards of Setting Big Goals

Hope on its own doesn't create
change. Action does.
—Lead Like a PIRATE

So often, I work at teaching my two children all they need to know that I forget how much they can teach me. It never ceases to amaze me the awe that my two daughters find in the simple things in life. On our spring break trip to a small amusement park, a simple picture reminded me of the emotions we experience when we try new things.

To me, the car ride designed for toddlers was anything but intimidating. It was brightly colored with a predictable track and slow speed, perfect for my daredevil two-year-old daughter. She eyed it from far away and eagerly got in line to try it. As we approached the line, she held my hand with a mix of excitement and visible trepidation. She surveyed the ride and monitored the looks on the faces of the kids already riding, as well as the speed of the cars.

When we got on the ride, she followed the safety protocol: "Buckle up, mommy!" As the ride began, her responses shifted at every turn from jubilation to nervousness. She threw her hands up in the air at the straightaways and cowered at the turns when it went just a little faster than she anticipated. I don't know how, but my husband perfectly captured the look on her face in the picture he took: utter terror and complete excitement at the same time.

When the ride slowed to a stop, she looked up at me with her eyes wide with excitement and said, "That was awesome!"

Her reaction reminded me so much of the power of taking risks and trying new things. Fear of the unknown is not without its emotional risks. But as I watched her exit the ride, I was reminded that taking risks also opens us to the potential for extreme joy, satisfaction, and reward.

Think of all we can accomplish if we remember and apply this simple truth to education. Think about the amazing results we can have in our schools and classrooms if we are able to overcome the initial worry, trepidation, or fear of trying something new: a new tech tool, a new flexible seating arrangement, a new strategy for connecting kids to outside experiences, a new way to collaborate and look at data, a new way to grow professionally, a new way to assign homework or give grades, a new way to do something *new*!

My two-year-old reminded me that although experiences can be scary, they can be fun, engaging, and, most importantly, worth the risk!

Change or innovation in a school setting can seem intimidating, but we must embrace change and seek opportunities to improve and move our schools forward. A key goal of any school should be to create an environment that promotes lifelong literacy. I am not talking about just on paper or in a school-improvement plan or through the delivery of the reading curriculum to meet the standards, but in a way that deepens a love of books and enhances a child's life as a reader.

Building a culture of readers is an important thread to assimilate into your greater school goals and branding. Weave it into the fabric of your school's improvement plan, goals, mission, and vision.

Develop a Classroom Learning Community of Readers

Engaging students in continuous improvement efforts at the classroom level begins on day one of the school year as students develop their own reading mission statement and goals. This process sets the stage for dynamic classroom collaboration, student engagement, student ownership, and accountability toward these goals.

As the school year progresses, students and teachers collaboratively write classroom goals and individual student goals. These goals are displayed in classroom data centers and student data binders, should align to building goals, and are communicated through the district, building, and classroom strategic plans. These goals are monitored through professional learning communities with teachers and during classroom meetings facilitated by students and in individual reading conferences. The power of the conversations that occur in professional learning communities and classroom meetings drive continuous improvement efforts and deeply embed the value of reading. Students communicate this progress to families during student-led conferences.

Build Goals with the Team

When I married my husband, it was no secret that I was marrying into a family of Iowa Hawkeyes and that the expectation of the family was to assimilate my allegiances, wear black and gold, and cheer for the Hawks as well. There have been some amazing seasons in which I am proud that I am a Hawkeye, even if just by marriage. As I watched the 2015 football team make school history by going 10–0 for the first time ever, I reflected on the practices that make strong sports teams successful and their application in school settings.

1. **A winning team made up of talented and committed individuals promotes positive culture**. Individuals are deeply dedicated to self-improvement as well as a cohesive team structure. Teachers in successful educational settings are also fully engaged in individual self-improvement and professional improvement while advocating and supporting the successes of their colleagues. Administrators and teachers who are lead readers promote reading at all levels of the school. They hold conversations about books, read both children's literature and professional titles, and take ownership of their professional learning related to literacy.

   Teachers and administrators who assume the role of a learner are first open to learning new strategies and sharing best practices with their peers. This comes in the form of classroom teachers presenting their learning during professional learning opportunities, teachers opening the doors of their classrooms so that colleagues can observe best practices, or a team of teachers nominating another team for an award to honor their collaboration. Just as a highly successful football team relies on positive culture, so do schools and educators.

2. **Fans and cheerleaders that encourage and support the team are vital to success**. High-functioning schools have high engagement of their families and communities just as sports teams have great interactions and support of their

fan base. Supportive families and engagement can lead to a variety of positive outcomes in the school setting. Encourage families to be part of the reading culture in your building. Invite parents to lead conversations about books with students. Recognize readers by making positive phone calls home and sharing student reading success. Ask parents to come in to conduct read alouds. Solicit donations from parents, local businesses, and the community for books. Families and parents are the biggest fans of our students. They are vital to the success in building a culture of readers in schools.

3. **A head coach and other leaders provide vision and support for the players to execute plays and make history**! Principals are essential to fostering a culture that supports vision and mission and provides support for this to become a reality. As a college football coach coordinates putting key players in essential positions, provides feedback, and orchestrates plays, he also places trust in the capable hands of his players to execute this vision on the field. Administrators need to hire educators with a strong conviction to read. Principals can accelerate the culture of readers through communicating their vision and branding a culture of readers. Principals and other administrators function in much the same way by placing teacher leaders in key roles, articulating vision, and monitoring progress.

4. **A strong and identifiable brand is formed and communicated throughout the community**. On home game nights, tens of thousands of Hawkeyes fill Kinnick Stadium dressed in black and gold with Hawkeye logos and University of Iowa trademarks. The team's progress is continuously updated on social media, and important information is released on its

website. Fans from all around the country tune in to watch the game. Schools can benefit from these practices as well with a glass classroom approach that shares important learning goals, activities, and information through social media, blogs, websites, and other communication sent to the home. Communicating the school brand shares positive stories of learning, student accomplishments, and teacher successes and is identifiable to students, parents, boards of education, and the community.

When the Hawkeyes won that the game in 2015 that put them at 10–0, they marched across the field, united in solidarity to retrieve the trophy. The trophy marked yet another win against a rival team but also signified the victory that was a function of hard work, individual success, a positive team dynamic, a cohesive group effort, strong leadership, and active and supportive fans. We can have that in the school setting as well as we lead our teachers and students to educational victory toward common and meaningful goals in a positive and supportive school culture with four key components:

A. A dedicated and *professional team of teachers, administrators, and support staff* who understand how their individual roles contribute to the success of the school as a whole. This means ensuring that students are in literature-rich learning environments that support creating a love of reading, regardless of the teacher they have.

B. *Parents and community members* who support the school, the students, and all learning endeavors through volunteerism and financial support of reading initiatives.

C. *Leaders* who are readers and who foster vision and a mission that places a priority on literacy.

D. An identifiable brand communicated efficiently to engage families and the community that includes an unwavering commitment to developing a culture of readers.

In an age that is focused on data-formed instruction, we need to focus school goals to reflect the vision and mission statements on school-improvement plans. Many schools strive to develop "lifelong learners" or "globally aware citizens" or "respectful and responsible students." When setting reading goals, we need to consider how the qualitative measures of reading can be used in setting school goals. Instructional leadership teams should consider more than just student achievement data when developing their school improvement plans. Some questions to consider as a leadership team:

- In what ways do we want our students to grow as readers?
- In what ways are our school goals supported through classroom goals and individual student goals? This cohesive and collaborative correlation not only provides a sense of purpose for the students and teachers but also provides a platform in which the school can communicate to the community what is important.
- In what ways can we involve our students in developing meaningful goals?

Brand the Vision

Goals that are monitored and reviewed are more likely to be met. Setting a goal to create a culture of readers is the first step. Next, you must develop and support a brand that communicates that goal. Develop a school motto or mantra that is easy to remember and say it often. We are the Royals. It reminds students to "Respect Others, Respect Yourself, and Respect Learning." Ensure they hear that *every day*. At the conclusion of morning announcements, students chant,

"Go be a Royal!" When they leave the office or I see them in the hall they hear, "Go be a Royal." This small gesture embeds that culture and sense of community in their spirit. Royals are readers, which is a non-negotiable.

Communicate your school mission and goals simply. A plan on a page details vision, values, and beliefs and should be displayed in all rooms and areas. Live and breathe the goals and refer to them consistently. When we put "develop a culture of readers" as the first item in our plan, it wasn't just words. It was followed by action and a key piece to our brand as a building.

Create a school hashtag and include it on school social media posts. (I am assuming you already have social media accounts for your school . . . if not, start now!) It can be simple, but make sure to communicate it and encourage frequent use. Consider a hashtag specific to the reading endeavors of your building. Use that hashtag to showcase the learning and reading of your school in various ways. Brand reading in your school by developing a specific hashtag for book talks, book recommendations, or #bookshelfies.

Leaders are storytellers of their schools, and sharing activities and events builds social capacity, a sense of community, and engages parents and the community in the learning process. Be cognizant of highlighting reading in unique ways when you are telling your story. Take and share pictures of the following:

- Students in the library
- Students exchanging books
- Stacks of new books donated to your school or purchased for your library
- Students engaging in independent reading time
- Staff doing a read aloud
- Infographics of teachers' favorite memories of reading
- Data of reading scores and achievement

Create a logo and make sure it is *everywhere*: the walls, letterhead, newsletters, social media posts, awards, the front door, bathroom mirrors, stickers, school signage, cafeteria menus, and on *everything*! We have them on everything from our flower pots outside to our laptops and soap dispensers!

Make sure your school colors are prominent and embedded in all elements of the school environment. When you look down the hallways, consider the banners, paint color, and decor. Does it match your school's colors and identity? Consider ways that you can incorporate your school colors in collaborative seating in the hallway and common areas. Ensure that your school goals are promoted through the common spaces. We have a passion to develop a culture of readers, so yellow bookcases and blue bookcases are found throughout the halls, and a bathtub of books painted in school colors is displayed in the entry way. This also includes ensuring ample access to books and opportunities to read throughout the school environment.

Greet families and students when they walk in the door with a gallery display of students dressed in school colors showcasing the important aspects of your school culture. Be sure to include pictures of students reading and celebrating books in these displays.

The details matter, and you can find unique ways to showcase your pride in your school. As a Royal, I am always on the lookout for items with books or crowns and find them in unexpected places. Mugs, signs, pens, decor, pencil pouches, and other items that I carry with me or use to decorate my space reiterate the importance of reading in my life.

Consider yourself as a mechanism for relaying your brand. Wear your school colors frequently and not just on spirit days. To promote reading, do you have T-shirts, ties, or funky socks that showcase your favorite books, reading, or characters? If you do, wear them frequently. If you don't, consider how you can physically promote reading through your attire.

Take your mascot and hide him around the school. Have the students find him and enjoy their squeals of excitement when they do. Make sure that he is found reading, checking out new books in the library, or recommending a new book. Print off copies of your mascot and encourage students to take them on trips and adventures with them *a la* Flat Stanley. Make sure a school hashtag corresponds with their posts. Challenge students to take pictures at literacy-based areas around the community, such as the library, coffee shops, bookstores, newsstands, or Little Free Libraries. Our school mascot, Crownie, has been to Space Camp, on a Disney Cruise, skiing in Colorado, to the Lego Store in California, to professional football games, on an ATV, climbing trees, out to dinner, and even to the top of Mt. Kilimanjaro! It's as simple as students taking the picture of the mascot with them on their travels and adventures and posting them (or having their parents post them) to school social media accounts. If they prefer, parents are also welcome to email them to the school or send hard copies to display in the hallway. It's a simple way to connect students to learning, the school, and each other.

Ensure that student awards and incentives correspond to your logo and brand and that colors are cohesive and consistent. That includes treats, stickers, certificates, plaques, and trophies. When promoting a culture of readers, incentives and rewards should reflect this vision. Bookmarks, books, or reading certificates support this.

Set Personal Reading Resolutions

In addition to setting goals for your school and with your students, it's important to set reading goals for yourself. Whether you're ringing in a New Year or a new school year, make it a point to periodically reset and reboot goals, as well as reflect on progress toward previous goals.

I set my own reading resolutions to model reading for my staff and students. In the past, I have set goals to:

- read a professional book a month and blog about it
- read a particular series or author
- maintain a Goodreads account
- Read at least once a week to students during lunchtime
- Complete a Newbery Award Winner reading challenge
- Increase family "read to self" time
- Ensure books are made readily available throughout the school in areas other than classrooms and the library
- Consider other environments in the building to share professional reading materials with staff
- Recommend a book a month to a fellow administrator

Once you have set your reading resolutions, share them with your staff, students, and PLN. Remember that you're always setting the example as the lead learner and lead reader.

TREASURE FROM THE TRENCHES

As educators, we are often tasked with finding solutions. We encourage our students to problem-solve and ask staff to creatively tackle difficulties. So developing a culture of readers seems as if it should be easy.

To reach the desired outcome, consider the process. From the first book a child hears, to the one the child holds and turns the pages, to the first book a child reads—each step moves a child toward becoming a reader.

Many children enter our doors after experiencing these first steps. Even so, without these experiences, we can celebrate these milestones right along with the child. Developing a culture of readers begins with exposure to print and excitement for the adventures reading allows.

We must put books in the hands of our students and believe they are readers. We must model the love of reading through read alouds, guest readers, and collaboration with our school and public library.

At Jefferson Elementary in Morton, Illinois, we kick off the year with a school-wide Read-a-thon, asking our parents and community to partner with us in developing readers. We share books with our students on their birthdays and for prizes at school-sponsored events, including Book "Grand(parent)" Event, "Pop Your Top & Read," "Read Like the Wind Day," and "World Read Aloud Day." Our newly added

Little Free Library promotes reading with our students, families, and community. Our PTO generously provides books for our students in the leveled book room, the school library, and in our classrooms.

Once our students enter our doors, we surround them with books and the time to step into a good story. We choose our priorities. We have taken a lot of little steps on our journey to develop a culture of readers. What's next? We will take another step . . . we are not done yet!

—Kate Wyman (@kate_wyman), principal,
in Morton School District, Morton, Illinois

TREASURE FROM THE TRENCHES

I knew that if I wanted my students to become readers for life, I had to find ways to bring books to life. What better way to do that than with a *Teach Like a PIRATE* (TLAP) Day with events and activities all focused on a fun book? My first TLAP day was based on my love of the Dr. Seuss book, *Hooray for Diffendoofer Day*. The story of students learning in unique and innovative ways instantly spoke to me, and I wanted to find a way to show my students that fun is at the heart of learning. This, of course, meant I needed a costume identical to the main character, Mrs. Bonkers (thank goodness my mom can sew and make last-minute costumes), as well as parent volunteers to donate and assist me in teaching the Diffendoofer School subjects: laughing, smelling, listening, yelling, creating poodles out of noodles, and tying knots.

The goal of our TLAP Day was twofold: learning and fun. These two goals go hand in hand. And through the fun, my students discovered that learning how to think prepares them for life beyond our classroom. Our TLAP Diffendoofer Day also reaffirmed for me just how vital harnessing excitement for reading is. As a result, I developed three summer challenges for my students to keep the fun going:

- #IMWAYR (It's Monday, What Are You Reading): provided students with a platform to share books they were reading and see what their peers were reading

- Summer Bingo Card

- Summer Shelfie

    —Stefanie Pitzer (@stefaniepitzer), instructional technology coach, Dunlap School District #323

Read more about these reading strategies and more at Stefanie's blog abcs2phds.edublogs.org.

PIRATE Leader Resource

To learn more about hosting a TLAP Diffendoofer Day, head over to Stefanie Pitzer's classroom blog: abcs2phds.edublogs.org.

Reflect on the Risks and Rewards of Your Reading Goals

Leadership Treasure Hunt
(Find This)

Identify the ways reading goals are expressed in
your school improvement plan. Do those goals
include fostering a love of reading?

Navigating the Seas
(Think About This)

What will your reading resolution be? How
can you communicate that with others
and hold yourself accountable?

Charting the Course
(Take Action)

Bring books to the forefront of your school and
conversations. How can you brand your mission so that
your school community knows reading takes priority?

Share your thoughts and ideas!
#LeadLAP

EQUIP YOUR CREW TO BE READER LEADERS

A parent or a teacher has only his lifetime;
a good book can teach forever.

—Louis L'Amour

I started my principalship in 2012 just as *Teach Like a PIRATE* by Dave Burgess was released. I read it over Christmas break and my view on teaching and learning was transformed. That book was the spark that ignited a passion to provide engaging classroom instruction for my students and powerful professional learning for my teachers. For teacher appreciation week that year, all staff were gifted a copy of the book and the #TLAP movement was set in motion in our school. We used that book as a catalyst to spark student engagement with our staff meetings the following year. Two teachers led that initial "Teach Like a PIRATE" professional learning opportunity, and I knew then that if I was going to expect staff to engage their students at a high level, I needed to ensure that the professional development that I was providing them was engaging.

Building a culture of readers starts with providing staff with effective and engaging professional development on best practices related to literacy and reading. Teachers also need to have the time to share the books and learning they've experienced in order to truly promote a love of reading in their classrooms and among students. This can be accomplished through a variety of approaches and applied to any content area or school initiative based on the discussion questions or focus areas. Professional development should be both strategic and meaningful, so make time to balance the emotional and academic domains of teaching and learning. What follows are a few of the ways leaders can promote reading through professional development experiences.

Classroom Crawl

I am always amazed and energized when walking through the classrooms in my building—really in any school building. Educators put so much thought and attention to detail into their classrooms. Creating a student-centered, literature-rich learning environment that promotes student ownership requires considerable time and energy. Students benefit from their teachers' hard work and dedication—and so can everyone else when we take time to showcase the personalized elements and examples of best practice and innovation in our classrooms.

Just before the school year started, my entire staff participated in a Classroom Crawl. We walked from classroom to classroom to tour the learning environments the staff had created for their students. To make the most of the tour (for ourselves and our PLNs), everyone had a list of different components or elements to look for. As we toured each classroom, we tweeted examples of innovation, developing a culture of readers, teachers as learners, creativity, building relationships, and more.

The focus of a Classroom Crawl can be tied to any school improvement areas. When focused on literacy and reading, participants can look for:

- Comfortable and engaging reading spaces
- Teachers as readers
- Celebrating readers
- Student book recommendations or book talks
- Creative book displays
- Classroom library organization
- Student choice in books
- Ample access to books
- Independent reading stamina display
- Reading conference evidence
- Digital reading examples
- Seasonal book displays

My teachers enjoy showing off their classrooms and learning by examining the environments of their peers in anticipation for the first day of school. This interactive option for PD got them moving, learning, collaborating with each other, and celebrating the positive elements of our school, including literacy and reading.

Speed Dating PD

As a principal, I am always seeking new ways to engage my staff in professional conversations and learning. So after talking with a friend about her speed-dating experience, I had a light-bulb moment: speed dating PD! During this professional learning approach, I paired teachers in two parallel rows and posed questions related to our school goals and school improvement plan. After each question, teachers rotated, and a new reflection question was posed. Our speed-dating PD activity included eight questions to be discussed in three-minute rounds (totaling about thirty minutes), and the rounds or number of questions could be shortened or lengthened to accommodate the focus area or time constraints.

This approach was successful for many reasons.

1. Cross-curricular and multi-grade-level discussion offered staff members exposure to varied perspectives and points of view.

2. Staff members shared unique ideas with colleagues outside their PLCs.

3. Support staff, student teachers, new teachers, and veteran teachers all participated at equal levels.

4. The sharing of meaningful ideas and activities motivated and empowered staff.

5. Everyone got involved in an active-learning, participation-required discussion.

Questions posed included:

1   As an educator, what book character are you most like and why?

2.   What is your favorite classroom read aloud?

3.   How will you get your students to have more "voice" and take center stage with reading in your classroom?

4.   Parent communication is key. How will you provide a back stage pass into your classroom reading activities this year?

5. You're all members of VIP PLCs. How will you ensure your time together is an effective jam session focused on developing a culture of readers?

6. Every rock star needs an entourage. What strategies will you use to foster a classroom learning community?

7. Time for special effects. What technology application or idea are you excited to use this year to foster a culture of readers?

8. When the show is over, how do you ensure you have supported students as readers in your classroom?

Strangers in a Ball Pit

Inspired by the video, "Strangers in a Ball Pit" created by Soul Pancake, I wanted to translate the effects of the experience in the ball pit to the staff in my building. In the video, two strangers sit and discuss question prompts written on various balls. Through the experience, they grow as a team, develop relationships, and communicate on a deeper level. Plus, sitting in a ball pit is fun, unique, and out of the norm for most adults.

So with a baby pool and plastic balls already in our storage room from our school carnival, I set to replicate the experience as an icebreaker at our staff meeting. The ball pit wasn't as big as the one from my inspiration, and the staff members weren't strangers, but we did learn a lot about one another.

As teachers or staff members sat in the ball pit, they pulled questions that were written on each ball and prompted answers from their partners. Questions included light-hearted subjects to get to know one another and literacy related topics focused on sharing strategies and best practices. Some questions included:

• What is your favorite read aloud?

- How do you get students excited about reading?
- What is your favorite picture book?
- What do you do to create a learning environment that promotes reading?
- How do you organize your classroom or school library to maximize student ownership and access to books?
- What's your proudest moment as a teacher?
- Why did you become a teacher?
- How do you de-stress after a challenging day?
- What are you most passionate about?
- What content area, skill, or concept do you enjoy teaching the most?
- What is your favorite technology tool to use in the classroom?
- How do you connect your students to others outside the walls of your classroom?
- If money were no object, what would you want to add to your classroom to improve student learning and engagement?
- What literacy-based website do you visit most frequently?
- Use only one word to describe your classroom.
- What is one thing you would want the public to know about teaching?

Some questions were also just plain silly to bring some laughter and levity to our experience:

- Would you rather be hairy or bald?
- What would you name your yacht if you had one?
- What's the first thing you do when you wake up in the morning?
- What would the title of the book based on your life be?

- If your personality was an animal, what would it be?

The ball pit icebreaker was a perfect introduction to our staff meeting. With a little humor and fun, we learned about one another's literacy practices and lives.

Flip a Staff Book Study

Let's face it, we are all busy. Reading and discussing books is an important aspect of developing a positive school teaching and learning culture, but time can be tight and gathering everyone together to discuss a book at the same time and place can be a challenge. Flipping a book study digitally can be a great option to amplify teacher voice, increase engagement, and provide opportunities for participation at a time and place that works for each individual staff member.

I read *Ditch That Textbook* by Matt Miller early in 2016. It only took me a short time to finish, and in that time, I had highlighted sections and marked the pages with sticky notes. I knew I had to share this book with my staff.

With our professional learning days accounted for and the end of the year approaching, I decided to launch a Twitter-based summer book study that teachers participated in on a voluntary basis. I sent out an email and was floored that the majority of my staff wanted in! We extended the invite to several other teachers from our professional learning network, and before we knew it, we had our staff collaborating with teachers across the country on the topic of revolutionizing their classrooms!

The first week focused simply on introductions. Teachers shared their titles and posted a selfie of themselves with the book. Using a hashtag for the book study made it easy to get acquainted and dip our toes into the Twitter book study waters.

The remaining weeks of the book study each focused on one chapter of the book. Throughout the study, we shared our favorite educational book titles, hashtags to follow, digital resources, and more. We also set goals for integrating technology in meaningful ways in the fall. Some of the goals listed included holding mystery Skype sessions, conducting Twitter chats with authors, using HyperDocs, and motivating students with digital badges. It was uplifting to see many hearts and retweets connected to the book study group's posts and ideas. I embedded some digital badges in the study to recognize those who participated. At the conclusion of the study, they were awarded a participation certificate.

It was empowering to see how many educators sought to be connected and learn through the summer months. In *Ditch That Textbook,* Matt discusses a few of the reasons why it's important for educators to be connected, including inspiration, motivation, challenge, camaraderie, apps, humor, and collaboration. Each of those elements was evident during the book study. As teachers used their time on vacation to learn and grow, they filled their teacher tool belts and learned how to make their classrooms better places to teach and learn.

Flipping a book study provides learners with opportunities to reflect and complete assigned readings and posts on their own time and terms while growing and learning from others. Building a culture of readers means teachers are learners as well.

Book Bingo

Whereas the previously discussed PD approaches can be applied to any content area or school-improvement area, I also *love* meetings centered specifically on engaging teachers in talking about books. I want to build the capacity of my staff to be reading teachers for the simplest and purest reason—to increase their knowledge of books that have touched the lives and hearts of their colleagues. "Book Bingo" is the perfect activity to accomplish that goal.

For the Book Bingo activity, each staff member brought a title, series, or author to share with colleagues at the staff meeting. They came prepared with the book and a short one-to-two-minute summary of the book and why they chose it. Through sharing, staff built a repertoire of titles to add to their classroom libraries as resources or read alouds.

As teachers talked about their books, they asked questions, made text-to-text connections, and grew their knowledge of titles and genres that they could refer to as recommendations to another child, teacher, or parent. These books included graphic novels, series, award-winning picture books, humorous read alouds, books that promote empathy, titles that dug into deeper emotional concepts, and more. Several times I heard, "That reminds me of another great title," or "You should read this book," or "Can I borrow that for my classroom," and "I need to add that to my personal reading list."

Every book title shared was recorded on a white board, and individual teachers wrote the titles at random on a blank bingo board. By the time everyone had shared their book, the bingo cards were filled, and it was time for a quick game of Book Bingo. At random, I called out the titles of books we had discussed. The beauty was that all teachers were winners and were able to select new titles of books for their classroom libraries as they left the meeting, thanks to donations from individual parents and our PTO. No words from a teacher make a principal happier than, "I love getting new books for my classroom!"

Book Tasting

I read a blog post from *The Four O'Clock Faculty*, which was just the inspiration I needed to share my professional library with my staff and continue to support the development of our culture of readers.

With the inspiration, I was ready to implement and make the idea work for my staff and building. The goals were simple:

1. Provide staff exposure to a variety of engaging, education-related, professional books in multiple content areas and genres.

2. Allow teachers to individualize their professional development journey by providing them with the opportunity to select a book from the given options to have purchased for them.

3. Create an atmosphere where educators are discussing and sharing their favorite book titles and offering further reading recommendations.

4. Support a community of teachers that demonstrate that everyone is a learner and everyone is a teacher.

I then set the stage to engage teachers in an informal, yet structured, learning experience designed to also model for them how to implement a book tasting within their classroom.

The set up included:

1. A table for each genre or content area

2. A hostess stand where staff placed their final orders

3. Snacks and goodies like any true bistro

4. Signage for each table, snack table, and door

The menu included books from five different content areas/genres:

1. Technology

2. Math

3. Literacy

4. Engagement and Innovation

5. Fiction

The staff was invited to record their favorite titles on a small bookmark that I created for them to take notes. A reflection napkin was provided for teachers to take notes regarding any conversations or ideas they had as they sampled the books. A final order form for teachers to record their selections was also included. These were all made available as they entered the room.

After a brief introduction and welcome, staff were asked to visit each table and sample the displayed and labeled books there, according to content area.

Teachers reflected and shared their thoughts on the books with their colleagues by flipping through the book, reading the back covers, or hearing feedback from peers who had already read the book. They were then asked to place an order for their individualized professional development selection by circling their choice and returning it to the hostess stand. I then placed an order for each teacher to receive their selection to add to their professional library. I also made it known that any of the books that were shared were already a part of our school library or my professional library, and they could borrow other books in addition to the one purchased for them.

Some reflections and thoughts from my experience:

1. A follow-up meeting with staff after they have time to read their selections could include a round up and book talk in which each staff member shares their reflections and take-aways from their books.

2. A follow-up meeting could also include a book exchange in which teachers trade or share their books with other teachers.

3. Staff can share how they chose to implement book tastings in their classroom.

Host a Literacy-Focused EdCamp

Professional development events are powerful places of connection and collaboration. So it isn't surprising that a fellow administrator and I decided to host our district's first EdCamp while at a tech conference. We shared a passion for individualized learning and understood the need to give more access to PD based on best practice, so we put a date on the calendar for a regional EdCamp, and the rest was history.

EdCamps have gained in popularity among educators as authentic, differentiated, and participant-driven forms of professional learning. They require a limited amount of logistical planning and yield amazing results in collaboration and professional growth. Here are five easy steps for hosting your own successful EdCamp:

Communicate

During a two-hour planning meeting in my office, my collaborator and I created a Google site, Canva graphic, Facebook invite, and email flier that we immediately sent out to our internal staff, principals in our region, and our regional office staff. The site included a Google form that we used to collect RSVPs so that we could plan for seating, food, and swag. In the time leading up to the event, we included email blasts, blog posts, and tweets to gain participants and spread the message.

Authenticate

EdCamps can be easily authenticated and supported by the EdCamp Foundation. Visit their website at edcamp.org/organize and register your EdCamp. This relatively easy process can result in the organization financially supporting the event to cover food, prizes, or other costs, as well as swag to give to participants. We received pens, buttons, stickers, magnets, sticky notes, markers, and more for our EdCamp by authenticating our event. In addition to officially registering our event, we made professional development hours available for participants. Whereas many of our registrants might have participated without these professional hours being awarded, this added incentive for attending. We also created an environment that showed attention to detail. Tablecloths, signage, food, centerpieces, and additional details demonstrated that this was a valid learning opportunity for teachers and staff to grow with one another and validated their professional aspirations and roles.

Collaborate

The key aspect of an EdCamp is that it is participant driven. Topics are not pre-created and rely on the attendees to develop. We gave participants time to generate a list of topics and then organized the suggestions to determine conversation groups. While in discussion groups, facilitators among the group worked through the questions and topics to share and discuss strategies and ideas that were of interest to participants.

Accelerate

One traditional element of an EdCamp is the "Sucks vs. Rocks" activity, which uses a Likert scale. Participants are given a topic that requires them to move across the room based on their opinions. At our EdCamp, we reserved this activity for the last hour to allow for movement and whole group conversation. Participants discussed ideas that included textbooks, flexible seating, and social media. Literacy-based topics could include:

- Picture books in the upper grades
- Banned books
- Digital books
- Assessment
- Reading logs
- Student choice in reading
- Audiobooks

To accelerate the EdCamp experience, we established a hashtag and encouraged participants to tweet and follow it. These tweets were also displayed on a central monitor using Tweet Monsters during the event.

Celebrate

Celebrating takes many forms. We celebrated the success of the day with individualized participant certificates and raffle prizes. When we advertised our EdCamp, we were surprised with authors and organizations that reached out and were willing to donate books, swag, or prizes for the day. The details of the day do matter and supported our mission of celebrating teachers and learning. There's no right or wrong way to EdCamp. The power comes in bringing professionals together in meaningful ways to grow and learn together.

Reflect on Literacy-Focused PD Opportunities for Your Crew

Leadership Treasure Hunt
(Find This)

What recent opportunities have you provided staff to discuss best practices in reading? How do you model best practices in reading instruction for your staff?

Navigating the Seas
(Think About This)

How can you take a pop culture phenomenon and apply it to how you deliver professional development?

Charting the Course
(Take Action)

Plan a professional learning opportunity that models classroom teaching strategies while engaging educators in discussions on books and literacy.

Encourage Reading at Home, on the Go, Everywhere!

Books are the plane, and the train, and the road. They are the destination, and the journey. They are home.
—Anna Quindlen

Any school leader knows the importance and power of engaging parents in the learning process. Parents can and should be our biggest allies in developing a strong school culture that is student-focused and conducive to building readers. As the professionals in our field, we are well-versed in best practices, strategies, and literature related to reading. Sharing what we are learning and doing, as well as the resources we are using, can empower parents to make reading part of their family culture. Here are a few ways to make sure the message about reading gets home.

Highlight Books at PTO Meetings

Talk about books and reading with parents whenever you can. One reoccurring opportunity is during PTO meetings. Dedicate a two-minute segment on the agenda to talk about what you are reading. I include a professional book and a children's book each month as part of my dedication to sharing my reading life.

When showcasing a professional book, I tie in the leadership impact during my comments. I share what I have learned and how this translates to our school community. I feel it is important for my families to know the value I place on reading and that I am constantly seeking ways to grow and improve my craft. Sharing these can spark positive conversations to build capacity for parents as leaders in our schools as well.

By sharing the books I'm reading, I demonstrate my focus on literacy, reading, and innovative practices in our school. I am cognizant and strategic when sharing books related to developing character and empathy prior to kindness week or about understanding the impact of screen time and developing digital citizenship when deploying 1:1 computer devices. If we are introducing a new curriculum initiative, I share related book titles. This provides resources for parents and helps me stay current on best practices, strategies, and research.

But I don't want school to seem like all work and no play, so I also highlight a recent or favorite children's book. I love sharing new titles or series that parents can jot down and consider reading with their children at home. These titles are often new releases, award winners, or books that focus on a character trait or theme that resonates with me. I might choose to share a new book in our school library or a recently published book. When possible, I also raffle off or provide copies of books at these meetings.

Parents as Readers

In chapter five, I talked about the need for children (and adults) to have access to books in the event of reading emergencies. When my daughter fractured her ankle after just a little too much fun on the trampoline, we suddenly experienced a reading emergency at home. As we came home from the doctor's office, her only choices for entertainment, due to her mobility constraints, were to read or color. She chose reading as she often does. I don't drill her with flashcards, sight word practice, letter tiles, or word walls; rather, we foster a love of reading in our house. Watching her read during that literal emergency caused me to reflect on how all parents can develop readers at home. (You'll notice that many of the same principles apply at school.) As lead readers in our school, we can provide information to our families that encourage authentic opportunities for students to grow as readers at home and provide books to students through the resources in our schools.

1. **Children need to have access to a variety of books**. The shelves in our home are filled with book titles that span a variety of genres, reading levels, and topics. The shelves are not centered in one particular location; rather, they are scattered throughout the house. Our children have access to a wide range of reading material in the living room, basement, toy room, and their bedrooms. We even have a bin of books in the middle of the backseat for car rides and keep a book stashed in the backpack for reading emergencies in the car or at school. Our bookshelves aren't pretty and organized by genre; our children are free to read a book, replace it in a location, and are often the first to be able to locate a particular title. Reading materials include board books that my eight-year-old confidently reads to her three-year-old sister, as well

as *Highlights* magazines, picture books, and beginner chapter books. It's okay if your child goes through a *Fly Guy* phase or loves all the books in the *Clifford* series. In fact, I just ordered a few more books in the *Mercy Watson* series, as it recently became a new favorite of ours. It's okay (and, in fact, it's awesome) if your child loves to re-read the same book over and over. Those behaviors and reading choices lay the foundation for developing an independent reader.

Babies and toddlers also benefit from access to a variety of books. Our youngest daughter loves pulling her older sister's books off the shelves and thumbing through the pages as much as she loves looking at pictures and connecting them to words in board books.

If you could look closely at the bookshelves throughout our home, some of my reading material has also made its way to these shelves, and although they don't read the words or understand the content in these books yet, it leads to my next principle.

2. **Children need to see models of lifelong learning and reading in the adults in their lives**. Just as often as I sit and read a book to my daughter or have her read a book to me, I sit beside her while we each read our own books and then talk about what we're reading. My husband and I consistently read the newspaper, articles, and mail in front of our children to model the importance of reading (and deciphering) non-fiction text.

3. **Children benefit from real-world experiences that they can make connections to as they read**. Those trips to the zoo, children's museum, or park are not only quality time spent as a family but also provide children with context as they read.

When they pull out a book, they can make important real-world connections and apply their individual experiences to the contents of the text. Our children enjoy going to many community events that build our bond as a family and that also develop their background knowledge to apply to their reading lives.

4. **Children need time to read, immerse themselves in books, and just enjoy reading**. It's so easy to fill our schedule with sports, activities, and events. All of these activities have tangible social and emotional benefits, but downtime that supports and encourages reading also provides value.

In our house, we try to reserve the time before bed as our sanctuary for reading. Additionally, we make sure we have access to books for reading in the car on the way to and from all of life's activities. We try not to make reading a chore but rather a time together that we look forward to and enjoy on a regular and consistent basis. The goal is to make reading just as much of our daily schedule as dinnertime and bath time.

Parent Bob for Books

Literacy nights, PTO meetings, and curriculum-focused parent evenings are the perfect time to share new book titles with parents and get more books into the homes of students. When sharing opportunities for developing readers in the home, review ways parents could assist their child in choosing relevant and meaningful book titles. One way to do this is to have parents "bob for books" just as you would bob for apples—only without the water and the mess. Parents simply reach into a basket of books and pick out one to take home. Be intentional about your reasons for sharing the specific books with your families and explain why those titles were selected. Educate parents about the types of books available and how various genres can support different aspects of reading growth.

1. Balance your reading diet with a combination of fiction and non-fiction texts across genres.

2. Picture books might require higher levels of critical thinking and are appropriate to use across grade levels to engage learners in inferences of pictures, plot, and character development.

3. Texts that tell a strong story can also be great examples for other literary elements.

4. Graphic novels are popular, engaging, and appealing to readers. It is okay to encourage reading these.

5. The *Who Was* series provides students access to biographies at a grade- and age-appropriate level (whowasbookseries. com/who-was).

6. Accessing the Newbery and Caldecott honor lists can provide an instant list of award-winning books for their contribution to children's literature or illustrations.

7. Books written by the same author or included in the same series can provide students structure in character development or plot; however, some authors write texts that differ in theme, level, or content.

Harness the Power of Technology

Our school social media is frequently updated throughout the school year. When teachers and students are in the building, there is always an opportunity to share the ongoing learning or activities. I wanted to find a way to maintain our social media engagement during school holidays and breaks. Using social media as an avenue to do read alouds, promote reading challenges, or share book talks can engage students and families during these breaks, as well as throughout the school year.

FlipGrid Book Talks

FlipGrid provides a unique and engaging platform to promote reading in many ways. FlipGrid allows users to record short videos and populates them on a collaborative form to view and share. To promote reading, set up a grid for staff to record their favorite read alouds and share them on social media throughout the summer or over breaks. Enhance this by engaging students in the process and allowing them to record themselves reading their favorite books and share them as well. You can spotlight district office staff or seek submissions from parents or community members.

PIRATE
Leader Resource

info.flipgrid.com

FlipGrid can also effectively amplify student voice and engage learners through short video creation. You can use FlipGrid to have students engage in many literacy-based activities:

- Have students join a grid to share their favorite book titles through short book talks.
- Encourage staff to do a read aloud for students and share them on school social media.
- Allow students to reflect on their reading using FlipGrid.
- Provide students the option of using FlipGrid to share their personal writing pieces.
- Have staff share tidbits about how they engage their students in reading by recording a FlipGrid.

- Reach out to other schools or classrooms and have students share their reflections about a common title with others as reading buddies.
- Ask older students to record picture books for younger students.

Social Media Read Alouds. Go Live!

Looking for a way to engage your kindergarten students before school or to reach out to students on a snow day? Social media read alouds can be the perfect avenue. When students aren't in our buildings, we have to find creative ways to connect with them and continue to build a culture of readers. Social media can be an engaging and accessible avenue to share stories. Consider doing a Facebook LIVE video of a read aloud. Promote the event ahead of time by setting a designated time for parents and students to tune in. You can do this from your living room, office, or other location, or even while on vacation. The simplicity of a read aloud makes it easy to implement, and social media stories can be done for any topic, theme, or special event. Some ideas:

Celebrating School

- *The Principal from the Black Lagoon* by Mike Thaler
- *A Fine, Fine School* by Sharon Creech
- *Our Principal Promised to Kiss a Pig* by Kalli Dakos and Alicia DesMarteau

Celebrating Reading

- *Miss Malarky Leaves No Reader Behind* by Judy Finchler and Kevin O'Malley
- *The Word Collector* by Peter Reynolds

100th Day of School

- *Henry's 100 Days of Kindergarten* by Nancy Carlson
- *The Night Before the 100th Day of School* by Natasha Wing

Holidays and Special Events

- *The Night Before a Snow Day* by Natasha Wing
- *The Night Before Christmas*
- *The Night Before Summer Vacation*

State Testing

- *Testing Miss Malarky* by Judy Finchler
- *The Big Test* by Julie Danneberg

Reinforcing Empathy and Kindness

- *Llama, Llama and the Bully Goat* by Anna Dewdney
- *Each Kindness* by Jacqueline Woodson
- *Be Kind* by Pat Zietlow Miller
- *We're All Wonders* by R.J. Palacio
- *Bullies Never Win* by Margery Cuyler
- *Recess Queen* by Alexis O'Neil

Just for Fun

- *The Book with No Pictures* by B.J. Novak
- *The Legend of Rock, Paper, Scissors* by Drew Daywalt

Social Media Reading Challenges

As much as we need to provide independent reading time at school, we also need to promote reading time at home. Throughout the year, you can utilize staff social media pages to encourage reading at home. Here are some examples.

- Mother's or Father's Day: Challenge followers to post a picture of their student reading with their parent or special figure in their lives.
- Ask families to post their child's current book. Send out certificates or books for a randomly selected post as an incentive.
- Many families have an "Elf on the Shelf." Have some fun with it and ask families to post a picture of their elf reading.
- Reading in the Wild: Have families post pictures of students reading outdoors or at a park, zoo, or nature center.
- Reading undercover: Post a picture of students sneaking reading moments.
- Read and lead: Challenge students to read to a younger child or sibling and share their photos.

Chapter Reflection Questions

Leadership Treasure Hunt
(Find This)

When can you read aloud? Schedule some
time on your calendar for read alouds.

Navigating the Seas
(Think About This)

What is one way you can incorporate social media
to promote literacy and reading in your school?

Charting the Course
(Take Action)

In what ways will you engage parents in learning
experiences about books and literacy strategies?

GET ENTHUSIASTIC ABOUT READING!

I began to realize how important it was to be an enthusiast in life. He taught me that if you are interested in something, no matter what it is, go at it at full speed ahead. Embrace it with both arms, hug it, love it and above all become passionate about it. Lukewarm is no good. Hot is no good either. White hot and passionate is the only thing to be.

—Roald Dahl

In the early 2000s, an ad campaign was launched that suggested, "Great cheese comes from happy cows. Happy cows come from California." In a happenstance conversation with a staff member, we began talking about this slogan and how it might apply to school culture, teacher performance, and student engagement. (Although we live in Illinois, the teacher was headed home to Wisconsin for Thanksgiving break. Naturally, cows, dairy, cheese, came up in our conversation.) No matter where you live, I hope you can spin the slogan to say, "Great learning comes from happy teachers. Happy teachers come from (fill in the blank with your school)!"

Establishing a school culture that promotes teacher engagement and satisfaction rests on some basic tenets of school leadership:

- **Administrators need to remember what it was like to sit on the other side of the desk.** I was told this by a veteran educator who had served on his community's board of education as well. This advice came the week I accepted my first principalship. His advice has always focused my interactions and approach with staff. As principals, we are teachers first and must constantly remember what it is like to be a teacher.

- **Staff norms that are collaboratively developed, monitored, and celebrated are the core of staff interactions and efforts.** Our staff norms are focused and intentional mutually agreed commitments. They are displayed in common work areas, celebrated in weekly communications to staff in our Friday Focus, and the start of our leadership and faculty meetings. An area in the teacher's workroom provides an opportunity for teachers to use sticky notes to share examples of their colleagues modeling these norms.

- **Principals should model taking risks and support teachers as *they* take risks.** I am not talking about jumping out of an airplane or bungee jumping off a bridge; I would never be able to model that kind of risk-taking. I am referring to professional educational risks that push learning in the classroom and foster creativity and innovation. This may include trying a new strategy or lesson, using a different app or technology device, or thinking outside the box regarding an approach to classroom management. Some of the best memories our students will have in school are those times when teachers stepped outside their comfort zone and tried something new or did something unconventional. In order for this to happen, teachers need to feel secure in knowing their attempts in learning will be encouraged, supported, and celebrated. After all, we are modeling lifelong learning for our students and the notion that the word FAIL can represent "a first attempt in learning."

- **Recognition and support go a long way in validating teachers in their work and interactions with students and families**. As adults, we are motivated by positive affirmations and validation of our work. Just as our students benefit from positive praise, teachers do too. Recognition can be both formal and informal.

- **Hiring and mentoring practices should support ongoing learning**. The core of any positive staff culture is hiring the right individuals who will contribute to their culture and teaching environment. Hiring practices that include the teachers or staff members who will work directly with the new hire can improve collaboration, offer current staff members voice, and give a glimpse into culture for the potential new hire. Set the tone by making the expectation of collaboration, communication, and positive interactions clear in interviews.

- **A school that is student focused accepts responsibility for all learners**. As I write this, I really should place this at the top of the list. To foster a positive school culture, this tenet is paramount. The adults in the building need to accept ownership for all learners, not just the ones in their classes or under their supervision. Learning is a process that doesn't stop when a child leaves a classroom or grade level. Staff that realize this promote a student-first approach and work collaboratively to support all student learning.

Challenges, moments of frustration, or bouts of tension are bound to happen in any school. To move forward and grow there, you will experience stumbling points and growing pains. The bumps are what we climb on. What does matter is that teachers feel supported by their leadership and one another to weather the storms and look for the rainbows. After all, happy teachers make happy kids. Happy kids become productive readers and learners. Here are a few ways to lead by example and boost the enthusiasm in and for your school.

Positive Notes

Walking down the hallways of most schools, you will see examples of reading and writing. Many of the student samples will have teacher feedback on them. One of my favorite activities as a principal is to add a sticky note to the student work with a special message or piece of positive feedback. Recognize students as readers and writers. Making time to see and read their work validates them and lets them know you care. It is a simple, yet meaningful and effective, to build relationships with kids.

Twitter Dust

When I logged into Twitter for the first time, I had no idea of the trajectory my life would take. The value of Twitter is not in the tool but in the relationships and connections I have developed as a result. I find daily doses of inspiration and motivation in the people I learn from and connect with.

As I was scrolling through tweets at #LeadLAP, I saw an amazing idea from Beth Houf (@BethHouf), a coauthor of *Lead Like a PIRATE*. She shared the idea of leaving "Fairy Gotchas" to staff tweeting about her school and recognizing them with a note of appreciation and change to purchase a soda.

The goal is simple: publicly recognize and reward staff for being self-motivated learners by connecting and growing their personal learning network or celebrating their classroom activities and achievements using your school hashtag.

It is a quick and easy idea to implement and, for me, it came at the perfect time! I was seeking ways to honor my staff for the added work they do to learn and grow for the benefit of our students. With a quick search through images and a Word document that I whipped up, I was ready to go. I logged onto Twitter and scrolled through our hashtag, #dgsroyals, looking for examples of teachers celebrating and showcasing the work of their students and classrooms.

With plastic "Royal" wands left over from a previous activity and some candy, I made my rounds to leave some Twitter dust for those teachers who showcased their students and classrooms using our hashtag. The feedback was positive as teachers tweeted their sweet surprises.

With such feedback, I decided to spread some Twitter dust to other buildings in my district and staff that used our district hashtag, #323learns. Baggies filled with a note of appreciation, chocolate, glitter, and a wand were sent through interoffice mail to celebrate the tweets of colleagues across the district.

A little Twitter dust to recognize and celebrate the staff in our district for growing, learning, and connecting brought some joy and glitter to all our days while promoting the development of a PLN and sharing resources.

The same concept can be employed for recognizing readers in the school building. With a little fairy dust in hand, recognize staff and students for developing a culture of readers in unique or strategic ways. Leave a note of appreciation and a sweet treat when you see any of these literacy-focused feats:

- A teacher displaying what they are reading

- A staff member or student engaging in a reading emergency
- A staff member or student discussing book recommendations with their peers
- A staff member or student contributing to the Little Free Library or reading emergency shelves

Positive Phone Call Home

She saw the school's number flashing on the caller ID. She had received calls many times about her fourth-grade son before.

- "Your son pushed a friend at recess."
- "Your son chose to use inappropriate words at lunchtime."
- "Your son refused to comply with staff directions."

So it was no wonder that she answered the phone with, "What's wrong?" with a defeated and concerned tone in her voice.

The trajectory of that phone call changed when I said, "Your son is okay. He's actually in my office because he received a positive office referral. He has demonstrated success in reading and has modeled great attitudes and efforts in reading among his peers. You should be proud!" This student demonstrated a lack of skills in key behavioral areas, but he was a reader.

The brief silence was followed by a shriek of excitement. "Yay! I am so happy to hear that."

All the while, that child stood next to me, beaming with pride. I had called him down a few moments earlier. He entered the office much like his mom answered the phone. Defensive, he asked, "What did I do?"

With a smile on my face, I shared the positive referral I had received from a staff member with him. His smile was enough to make me tear up, and I almost lost it when he said, "My mom is going to be so proud!"

He was all smiles as he signed the Wall of Honor in the office. He beamed when I had him stand beside me as I made a phone call to his mom.

This all took a matter of minutes, but the impact lasted so much longer.

Celebrating the positive behaviors and accomplishments of our students is important for our students, their parents, and for us. Not only do students and parents love receiving positive feedback, but my mood instantly improved as I made the conscious decision to focus and promote the positive. And with every call you make as the school leader, you model what it means to promote the positive for your teachers.

Students who struggle behaviorally or socially might shine academically, and reading is a perfect area to recognize what they are doing right. All students can be celebrated for being readers. Staff can celebrate a great book choice, improvement in their reading goals, a choice to read independently or collaboratively, increased reading stamina, or willingness to model reading for other students.

Receiving a positive office referral and making encouraging phone calls home are highlights of my day. I enjoy recognizing and building the relationships with students who are leading examples in our school.

The process is simple:

1. A staff member sees a positive behavior or accomplishment.

2. A staff member completes a paper office referral form or Google Form submission that is sent to the office.

3. The student is recognized during the morning announcements.

4. The student is called to the office, where he or she is praised and celebrated and signs the Wall of Honor.

5. The principal calls the parent to share the great news.

6. The principal puts the kid on the phone with the parent.

7. Everyone does a happy dance!

In a school with focused goals and vision, these positive phone calls home can be strategically made based on specific criteria or accomplishments. I prefer to leave it open ended, but some of my favorite phone calls home are when I can discuss what a child is reading or the smart choices they made related to their reading time.

Reading Rewards

Reading can be celebrated in many ways. As students set goals and meet them, consider how you can celebrate their accomplishments and build enthusiasm for reading.

- Send them to the principal with a positive reading referral. Celebrate that positive reading referral by posting a picture on the school Facebook page or sending it home to parents.
- Share reading accomplishments in school or classroom newsletters or during morning announcements.
- Give them a handwritten note expressing your pride in their accomplishment.
- Give them a hug or high five.
- Have them ring a bell or sound a classroom alarm when they complete a book or meet a reading goal.
- Name them student of the month (if your school has one).
- Present them with a traveling class trophy that sits on their desk for a pre-determined amount of time.
- Make a positive phone call home while the student is standing with you. That's sure to make both the student's and the parent's day!

- Have the class give the student a special cheer.
  - Take their picture and email it to their parents when they meet a goal.
  - Eat lunch with individual students or small groups of students in the cafeteria or invite them to eat in the principal's office with a formal invitation.
  - Have a black-out day and use flashlights and LED lights to read.
  - Greet them at the door wearing a funny costume, hat, or shirt related to the book you're reading.
  - Allow a student to choose the classroom read-aloud book.
  - Let students read at spots around the room, under their desks, or other places that might typically be off-limits, like the teacher's lounge or principal's office.
  - Give them a special chair at their desk for the day. Paint an old stool, bedazzle an old rocking chair, or paint a used dining chair and then rotate it around classrooms.
  - Establish a classroom brag board. Place pictures of students on the board when they meet a goal or celebrate an accomplishment.
  - Allow students to earn the privilege of being a member of the classroom hall of fame. Hang their picture in a sacred spot that is never taken down.
  - Allow them to read with a buddy.
  - Allow them to read with a younger student.
  - Allow them to read with the principal.
  - Have a reading campout.
  - Read outside.
  - Put a button or name tag on them that says, "Ask Me Why I am a Cool Kid" or another special saying.
  - Put a button or name tag on them that says "Class VIP."

- Tweet their favorite author.
- Leave a sticky note of encouragement on their desk or in their planner.

Chapter Reflection Questions

Leadership Treasure Hunt
(Find This)

Who is the most enthusiastic reader on your campus?

Navigating the Seas
(Think About This)

Why is it important for adults to model enthusiasm in reading for their students? Why is it important for school leaders to model enthusiasm for staff?

Charting the Course
(Take Action)

In what small but meaningful ways can you show enthusiasm for reading in your school or classroom?

Concluding Thoughts: Lead the Way to Reading Treasure

Each book carries hidden treasures just waiting to be uncovered by an eager reader. Our jobs as leaders of reading in our buildings is to vigilantly and relentlessly work to create environments that allow our students and staff to find these treasures and to experience the wonder of reading.

I charge you to walk the plank and jump in purposefully and with intensity to ensure reading and literacy are truly the cornerstones of your vision and mission. When you model the school environment that you want to create through your words and actions, this vision and mission will come to fruition.

Create a treasure map throughout your school that ensures:

- A love of reading, and the importance that is placed on reading, is evident in displays and access to books when you walk through the halls. Showcase books everywhere!
- Students have equal and plentiful access to books and high-quality literature with no strings attached. Create a school environment that not only supports the development of readers but also magnifies the love of reading.
- Activities and events are strategically planned to promote a love of reading.

- Teachers and staff are active readers and model lifelong reading for students.
- Teachers are engaged in professional-learning activities that keep them current with book titles and best practices in reading instruction.

BIBLIOGRAPHY

Chapter 1

Casas, Jimmy. *Culturize: Every Student. Every Day. Whatever It Takes.* San Diego: Dave Burgess Consulting, Inc., 2017.

Chapter 10

Miller, Matt. *Ditch that Textbook: Free Your Teaching and Revolutionize Your Classroom.* San Diego: Dave Burgess Consulting, Inc., 2015.

ACKNOWLEDGMENTS

I started on my path as a lifelong learner the moment I walked into a kindergarten classroom as a five-year-old little girl. My parents have given me both the roots and wings needed to sail uncharted waters. I will be eternally grateful for their unwavering love and for instilling in me a love of learning that only continues to grow. They taught me to love learning.

I value each of the educators that grew my love of learning over the years in small and big ways and feel I would be remiss not to acknowledge their direct impact on my ability to actually write and publish a book. I am able to write these words and share my experiences thanks to the teachers I had as a student. I am forever grateful to Mrs. Halma, Mrs. Schermerhorn, Mrs. Fiantago, Mr. Wesley, Mr. Liggett, and Dr. Anotla-Crowe. Each of them taught me the value of learning and the power of building relationships with students.

When my path of lifelong learning took me to college, I met my husband, Brett. He continues to support my crazy ideas and wild dreams and encourage me along the way. He has taught me the power of a strong network and to embrace the learning process and allow the journey to open new doors.

I have been fortunate to be surrounded by supportive colleagues and friends who have boosted me in all phases of my career. Some, like Tony Ingold, took a chance in hiring a first-year teacher. Others, like Joe Sander, Todd Jefferson, and Greg Fairchild, mentored and encouraged me to pursue leadership challenges. I am fortunate to have others, like Marcus Belin, Stefanie Pitzer, and Lisa Kamin, that simply cheer me on. In each of their own ways, they have mentored me, challenged me, and pushed me to grow as an educator. They have taught me that to be a strong leader, you just have to remain focused on the kids, and everything else will fall into place.

In 2012, I walked into a grade school as principal for the first time. To the staff, students, and families at Dunlap Grade School, you are my second home. I get so much joy in building relationships with those in our school community and watching the students and teachers grow. I am so proud to be a DGS Royal and tell our story in this book. Our school has taught me the value in learning alongside the students and the importance of instilling a love of learning and creating a culture of readers.

I never learned as much as when I became a mom. My two girls, Lydia and Lauren, are an endless source of inspiration and motivation. I strive to be the best wife, mother, and educator possible because of them. They have taught me more than I will ever teach them! They have taught me the importance public schools play in developing the whole child. They have taught me the importance of looking at and approaching teaching, learning, and life through the eyes of a child.

Dave and Shelley Burgess and Beth Houf, you saw the potential in this book before I did. Thank you for giving me the opportunity to share my manifesto and encourage more educators to read like pirates. I am grateful for the opportunity and for your influence on my career and impact on my school and path as an educator. I am a stronger, happier, and more engaged educator because of you. You have each taught me the power in taking risks and sharing my passion.

Bring Mandy Ellis to Your School or District

Mandy Ellis is passionate about helping schools develop a positive culture with a focus on reading and literacy. She has presented at regional, state, and national conferences and workshops, as well as for online professional development programs. She provides practical and easy to implement strategies that inspire participants to make meaningful changes in their schools.

Presentations are individually prepared for your specific event, audience, and school on the following topics:

- Reading and Literacy
- Personalized Professional Learning
- Powerful Professional Development Strategies
- Promoting Positive School Culture

A few of Mandy's popular presentations include . . .

- Leading with Literacy: A Pirate Principal's Guide to Creating a Culture of Readers
- Set SAIL with School-Wide Literacy Strategies to Promote a Culture of Readers
- Ten Things Not to Do as a Principal
- Be the SPARK: Strategies to IGNITE Powerful Professional Learning
- Power UP and Personalize Your Own PD
- Empowerment through Engagement: Student Ownership in Conferences and IEPS

Connect with Mandy Ellis for more information about bringing her to your school event.

 @mandyeellis

✉ principalsdecree@gmail.com

🌐 PrincipalsDecree.com

MORE FROM DAVE BURGESS Consulting, Inc.

LEAD Like a PIRATE
Make School Amazing for Your Students and Staff
By Shelley Burgess and Beth Houf
(@Burgess_Shelley, @BethHouf)

   Lead Like a PIRATE maps out character traits necessary to captain a school or district. You'll learn where to find treasure already in your classrooms and schools—and bring out the best in educators. Find encouragement in your relentless quest to make school amazing for everyone!

Lead with Culture
What Really Matters in Our Schools
By Jay Billy (@JayBilly2)

   In this *Lead Like a PIRATE* guide, Jay Billy explains that making school a place where students and staff want to be starts with culture. You'll be inspired by this principal's practical ideas for creating a sense of unity—even in the most diverse communities.

Teach Like a PIRATE
Increase Student Engagement, Boost Your Creativity, and Transform Your Life as an Educator
By Dave Burgess (@BurgessDave)

   New York Times' bestseller *Teach Like a PIRATE* sparked a worldwide educational revolution with its passionate teaching manifesto and dynamic student-engagement strategies. Translated into multiple languages, it sparks outrageously creative lessons and life-changing student experiences.

Learn Like a PIRATE

Empower Your Students to Collaborate, Lead, and Succeed

By Paul Solarz (@PaulSolarz)

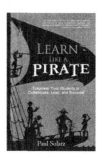

Passing grades don't equip students for life and career responsibilities. *Learn Like a PIRATE* shows how risk-taking and exploring passions in stimulating, motivating, supportive, self-directed classrooms create students capable of making smart, responsible decisions on their own.

P is for PIRATE

Inspirational ABC's for Educators

By Dave and Shelley Burgess (@Burgess_Shelley)

In *P is for Pirate*, husband-and-wife team Dave and Shelley Burgess tap personal experiences of seventy educators to inspire others to create fun and exciting places to learn. It's a wealth of imaginative and creative ideas that make learning and teaching more fulfilling than ever before.

eXPlore Like a Pirate

Gamification and Game-Inspired Course Design to Engage, Enrich, and Elevate Your Learners

By Michael Matera (@MrMatera)

Create an experiential, collaborative, and creative world with classroom game designer and educator Michael Matera's game-based learning book, *eXPlore Like a Pirate*. Matera helps teachers apply motivational gameplay techniques and enhance curriculum with gamification strategies.

Play Like a Pirate

Engage Students with Toys, Games, and Comics

By Quinn Rollins (@jedikermit)

In *Play Like a Pirate*, Quinn Rollins offers practical, engaging strategies and resources that make it easy to integrate fun into your curriculum. Regardless of grade level, serious learning can be seriously fun with inspirational ideas that engage students in unforgettable ways.

The Innovator's Mindset

Empower Learning, Unleash Talent, and Lead a Culture of Creativity

By George Couros (@gcouros)

In *The Innovator's Mindset*, teachers and administrators discover that compliance to a scheduled curriculum hinders student innovation, critical thinking, and creativity. To become forward-thinking leaders, students must be empowered to wonder and explore.

Pure Genius

Building a Culture of Innovation and Taking 20% Time to the Next Level

By Don Wettrick (@DonWettrick)

Collaboration—with experts, students, and other educators—helps create interesting and even life-changing opportunities for learning. In *Pure Genius*, Don Wettrick inspires and equips educators with a systematic blueprint for beating classroom boredom and teaching innovation.

Ditch That Textbook

Free Your Teaching and Revolutionize Your Classroom

By Matt Miller (@jmattmiller)

Ditch That Textbook creates a support system, toolbox, and manifesto that can free teachers from outdated textbooks. Miller empowers them to untether themselves, throw out meaningless, pedestrian teaching and learning practices, and evolve and revolutionize their classrooms.

50 Things You Can Do with Google Classroom

By Alice Keeler and Libbi Miller
(@alicekeeler, @MillerLibbi)

50 Things You Can Do with Google Classroom provides a thorough overview of this GAfE app and shortens the teacher learning curve for introducing technology in the classroom. Keeler and Miller's ideas, instruction, and screenshots help teachers go digital with this powerful tool.

50 Things to Go Further with Google Classroom

A Student-Centered Approach

By Alice Keeler and Libbi Miller
(@alicekeeler, @MillerLibbi)

In *50 Things to Go Further with Google Classroom: A Student-Centered Approach*, authors and educators Alice Keeler and Libbi Miller help teachers create a digitally rich, engaging, student-centered environment that taps the power of individualized learning using Google Classroom.

140 Twitter Tips for Educators

Get Connected, Grow Your Professional Learning Network, and Reinvigorate Your Career

By Brad Currie, Billy Krakower, and Scott Rocco
(@bradmcurrie, @wkrakower, @ScottRRocco)

In *140 Twitter Tips for Educators*, #Satchat hosts and founders of Evolving Educators, Brad Currie, Billy Krakower, and Scott Rocco, offer step-by-step instruction on Twitter basics and building an online following within Twitter's vibrant network of educational professionals.

Master the Media

How Teaching Media Literacy Can Save Our Plugged-In World

By Julie Smith (@julnilsmith)

Master the Media explains media history, purpose, and messaging, so teachers and parents can empower students with critical-thinking skills, which lead to informed choices, the ability to differentiate between truth and lies, and discern perception from reality. Media literacy can save the world.

The Zen Teacher

Creating Focus, Simplicity, and Tranquility in the Classroom

By Dan Tricarico (@thezenteacher)

Unrushed and fully focused, teachers influence—even improve—the future when they maximize performance and improve their quality of life. In *The Zen Teacher*, Dan Tricarico offers practical, easy-to-use techniques to develop a non-religious Zen practice and thrive in the classroom.

Your School Rocks . . . So Tell People!

Passionately Pitch and Promote the Positives Happening on Your Campus

By Ryan McLane and Eric Lowe (@McLane_Ryan, @EricLowe21)

Your School Rocks . . . So Tell People! helps schools create effective social media communication strategies that keep students' families and the community connected to what's going on at school, offering more than seventy immediately actionable tips with easy-to-follow instructions and video tutorial links.

The Classroom Chef

Sharpen Your Lessons. Season Your Classes. Make Math Meaningful

By John Stevens and Matt Vaudrey (@Jstevens009, @MrVaudrey)

With imagination and preparation, every teacher can be *The Classroom Chef* using John Stevens and Matt Vaudrey's secret recipes, ingredients, and tips that help students "get" math. Use ideas as-is, or tweak to create enticing educational meals that engage students.

How Much Water Do We Have?

5 Success Principles for Conquering Any Challenge and Thriving in Times of Change

By Pete Nunweiler with Kris Nunweiler

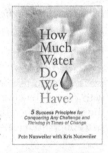

Stressed out, overwhelmed, or uncertain at work or home? It could be figurative dehydration.

How Much Water Do We Have? identifies five key elements necessary for success of any goal, life transition, or challenge. Learn to find, acquire, and use the 5 Waters of Success.

The Writing on the Classroom Wall

How Posting Your Most Passionate Beliefs about Education Can Empower Your Students, Propel Your Growth, and Lead to a Lifetime of Learning

By Steve Wyborney (@SteveWyborney)

Big ideas lead to deeper learning, but they don't have to be profound to have profound impact. Teacher Steve Wyborney explains why and how sharing ideas sharpens and refines them. It's okay if some ideas fall off the wall; what matters most is sharing and discussing.

Kids Deserve It!

Pushing Boundaries and Challenging Conventional Thinking

By Todd Nesloney and Adam Welcome
(@TechNinjaTodd, @awelcome)

Think big. Make learning fun and meaningful. In *Kids Deserve It!* Nesloney and Welcome offer high-tech, high-touch, and highly engaging practices that inspire risk-taking and shake up the status quo on behalf of your students. Rediscover why you became an educator, too!

LAUNCH

Using Design Thinking to Boost Creativity and Bring Out the Maker in Every Student

By John Spencer and A.J. Juliani (@spencerideas, @ajjuliani)

When students identify themselves as makers, inventors, and creators, they discover powerful problem-solving and critical-thinking skills. Their imaginations and creativity will shape our future. John Spencer and A.J. Juliani's *LAUNCH* process dares you to innovate and empower them.

Instant Relevance

Using Today's Experiences to Teach Tomorrow's Lessons

By Denis Sheeran (@MathDenisNJ)

Learning sticks when it's relevant to students. In *Instant Relevance,* author and keynote speaker Denis Sheeran equips you to create engaging lessons *from* experiences and events that matter to students while helping them make meaningful connections between the real world and the classroom.

Escaping the School Leader's Dunk Tank

How to Prevail When Others Want to See You Drown

By Rebecca Coda and Rick Jetter
(@RebeccaCoda, @RickJetter)

Dunk-tank situations—discrimination, bad politics, revenge, or ego-driven coworkers—can make an educator's life miserable. Coda and Jetter (dunk-tank survivors themselves) share real-life stories and insightful research to equip school leaders with tools to survive and, better yet, avoid getting "dunked."

Start. Right. Now.

Teach and Lead for Excellence

By Todd Whitaker, Jeff Zoul, and Jimmy Casas
(@ToddWhitaker, @Jeff_Zoul, @casas_jimmy)

Excellent leaders and teachers *Know the Way, Show the Way, Go the Way, and Grow Each Day*. Whitaker, Zoul, and Casas share four key behaviors of excellence from educators across the U.S. and motivate to put you on the right path.

Teaching Math with Google Apps

50 G Suite Activities

By Alice Keeler and Diana Herrington
(@AliceKeeler, @mathdiana)

Teaching Math with Google Apps meshes the easy student/teacher interaction of Google Apps with G Suite that empowers student creativity and critical thinking. Keeler and Herrington demonstrate fifty ways to bring math classes into the twenty-first century with easy-to-use technology.

Table Talk Math

A Practical Guide for Bringing Math into Everyday Conversations

By John Stevens (@Jstevens009)

In *Table Talk Math*, John Stevens offers parents—and teachers—ideas for initiating authentic, math-based, everyday conversations that get kids to notice and pique their curiosity about the numbers, patterns, and equations in the world around them.

Shift This!

How to Implement Gradual Change for Massive Impact in Your Classroom

By Joy Kirr (@JoyKirr)

Establishing a student-led culture focused on individual responsibility and personalized learning *is* possible, sustainable, and even easy when it happens little by little. In *Shift This!*, Joy Kirr details gradual shifts in thinking, teaching, and approach for massive impact in your classroom.

Unmapped Potential

An Educator's Guide to Lasting Change

By Julie Hasson and Missy Lennard (@PPrincipals)

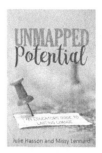

Overwhelmed and overworked? You're not alone, but it can get better. You simply need the right map to guide you from frustrated to fulfilled. *Unmapped Potential* offers advice and practical strategies to forge a unique path to becoming the educator and *person* you want to be.

Shattering the Perfect Teacher Myth

6 Truths That Will Help You THRIVE as an Educator

By Aaron Hogan (@aaron_hogan)

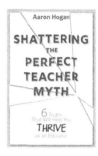

Author and educator Aaron Hogan helps shatter the idyllic "perfect teacher" myth, which erodes self-confidence with unrealistic expectations and sets teachers up for failure. His book equips educators with strategies that help them shift out of survival mode and THRIVE.

Social LEADia

Moving Students from Digital Citizenship to Digital Leadership

By Jennifer Casa-Todd (@JCasaTodd)

A networked society requires students to leverage social media to connect to people, passions, and opportunities to grow and make a difference. *Social LEADia* helps shift focus at school and home from digital citizenship to digital leadership and equip students for the future.

Spark Learning

3 Keys to Embracing the Power of Student Curiosity

By Ramsey Musallam (@ramusallam)

Inspired by his popular TED Talk "3 Rules to Spark Learning," Musallam combines brain science research, proven teaching methods, and his personal story to empower you to improve your students' learning experiences by inspiring inquiry and harnessing its benefits.

Ditch That Homework
Practical Strategies to Help Make Homework Obsolete
By Matt Miller and Alice Keeler (@jmattmiller, @alicekeeler)

In *Ditch That Homework*, Miller and Keeler discuss the pros and cons of homework, why it's assigned, and what life could look like without it. They evaluate research, share parent and teacher insights, then make a convincing case for ditching it for effective and personalized learning methods.

The Four O'Clock Faculty
A Rogue Guide to Revolutionizing Professional Development
By Rich Czyz (@RACzyz)

In *The Four O'Clock Faculty*, Rich identifies ways to make professional learning meaningful, efficient, and, above all, personally relevant. It's a practical guide to revolutionize PD, revealing why some is so awful and what you can do to change the model for the betterment of everyone.

Culturize
Every Student. Every Day. Whatever It Takes.
By Jimmy Casas (@casas_jimmy)

Culturize dives into what it takes to cultivate a community of learners who embody innately human traits our world desperately needs—kindness, honesty, and compassion. Casas's stories reveal how "soft skills" can be honed while exceeding academic standards of twenty-first-century learning.

Code Breaker
Increase Creativity, Remix Assessment, and Develop a Class of Coder Ninjas!
By Brian Aspinall (@mraspinall)

You don't have to be a "computer geek" to use coding to turn curriculum expectations into student skills. Use *Code Breaker* to teach students how to identify problems, develop solutions, and use computational thinking to apply and demonstrate learning.

The Wild Card

7 Steps to an Educator's Creative Breakthrough

By Hope and Wade King (@hopekingteach, @wadeking7)

The Kings facilitate a creative breakthrough in the classroom with *The Wild Card*, a step-by-step guide to drawing on your authentic self to deliver your content creatively and be the *wild card* who changes the game for your learners.

Stories from Webb

The Ideas, Passions, and Convictions of a Principal and His School Family

By Todd Nesloney (@TechNinjaTodd)

Stories from Webb goes right to the heart of education. Told by award-winning principal Todd Nesloney and his dedicated team of staff and teachers, this book reminds you why you became an educator. Relatable stories reinvigorate and may inspire you to tell your own!

The Principled Principal

10 Principles for Leading Exceptional Schools

By Jeffrey Zoul and Anthony McConnell
(@Jeff_Zoul, @mcconnellaw)

Zoul and McConnell know from personal experience that the role of a school principal is one of the most challenging *and* the most rewarding in education. Using relatable stories and real-life examples, they reveal ten core values that will empower you to work and lead with excellence.

The Limitless School

Creative Ways to Solve the Culture Puzzle

By Abe Hege and Adam Dovico (@abehege, @adamdovico)

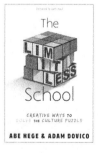

Being intentional about creating a positive culture is imperative for your school's success. This book identifies the nine pillars that support a positive school culture and explains how each stakeholder has a vital role to play in the work of making schools safe, inviting, and dynamic.

Google Apps for Littles

Believe They Can

By Christine Pinto and Alice Keeler
(@PintoBeanz11, @alicekeeler)

Learn how to tap into students' natural curiosity using technology. Pinto and Keeler share a wealth of innovative ways to integrate digital tools in the primary classroom to make learning engaging and relevant for even the youngest of today's twenty-first-century learners.

Be the One for Kids

You Have the Power to Change the Life of a Child

By Ryan Sheehy (@sheehyrw)

Students need guidance to succeed academically, but they also need our help to survive and thrive in today's turbulent world. They need someone to model the attributes that will help them win not just in school but in life as well. That someone is you.

Let Them Speak

How Student Voice Can Transform Your School

By Rebecca Coda and Rick Jetter
(@RebeccaCoda, @RickJetter)

We say, "Student voice matters," but are we really listening? This book will inspire you to find out what your students really think, feel, and need. You'll learn how to listen to and use student feedback to improve your school's culture. All you have to do is ask—and then *Let Them Speak*.

The EduProtocol Field Guide

16 Student-Centered Lesson Frames for Infinite Learning Possibilities

By Marlena Hebern and Jon Corippo
(@mhebern, @jcorippo)

Are you ready to break out of the lesson-and-worksheet rut? Use *The EduProtocol Field Guide* to create engaging and effective instruction, build culture, and deliver content to K–12 students in a supportive, creative environment.

All 4s and 5s

A Guide to Teaching and Leading Advanced Placement Programs

By Andrew Sharos (@AndrewSharosAP)

AP classes shouldn't be relegated to "privileged" schools and students. With proper support, every student can experience success. *All 4s and 5s* offers a wealth of classroom and program strategies that equip you to develop a culture of academic and personal excellence.

Shake Up Learning

Practical Ideas to Move Learning from Static to Dynamic

By Kasey Bell (@ShakeUpLearning)

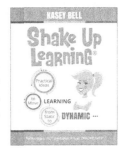

Is the learning in your classroom static or dynamic? *Shake Up Learning* guides you through the process of creating dynamic learning opportunities—from purposeful planning and maximizing technology to fearless implementation.

The Secret Solution

How One Principal Discovered the Path to Success

Todd Whitaker, Sam Miller, and Ryan Donlan
(@ToddWhitaker, @SamMiller29, @RyanDonlan)

An entertaining look at the path to leadership excellence, this parable provides leaders with a non-threatening tool to discuss problematic attitudes in schools. This updated edition includes a reader's guide to help you identify habits and traits that can help you and your team succeed.

The Path to Serendipity

Discover the Gifts along Life's Journey

By Allyson Apsey (@AllysonApsey)

In this funny, genuine, and clever book, Allyson Apsey shares relatable stories and practical strategies for living a meaningful life regardless of the craziness happening around you. You'll discover that you really do have the power to choose the kind of life you live—every day.

The Pepper Effect

Tap into the Magic of Creativity, Collaboration, and Innovation

By Sean Gaillard (@smgaillard)

Using *Sgt. Pepper's Lonely Hearts Club Band* by The Beatles as a template for inspiration, Sean Gaillard explores the necessary steps for creating the conditions for motivation, collaboration, creativity, and innovation in your schoolhouse.

The EduNinja Mindset

11 Habits for Building a Stronger Mind and Body

By Jennifer Burdis (@jennifer_burdis)

As a two-time *American Ninja Warrior* contestant, educator, and trainer, Jen Burdis pushes herself to physically and mentally overcome obstacles. In *The EduNinja Mindset*, Burdis shares her strategies to empower teachers, students, and families to develop healthy habits.

Sparks in the Dark

Lessons, Ideas, and Strategies to Illuminate the Reading and Writing Lives in All of Us

By Travis Crowder and Todd Nesloney
(@teachermantrav, @TechNinjaTodd)

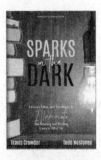

More standards, tests, and mandates are not the answer to improving literacy. *Sparks in the Dark* inspires educators in every subject area to be intentional about instilling a love of reading and writing in all students.

Be REAL

Educate from the Heart

By Tara Martin (@TaraMartinEDU)

REAL educators are relatable, they expose vulnerability by sharing their experiences, they are approachable, they learn through life. They are the heart of our schools. In *Be REAL*, you'll learn the power of being true to yourself and find the courage to teach from the heart.

ABOUT THE AUTHOR

Mandy Ellis is first and foremost a wife and mother with a passion for teaching and learning that is demonstrated in her job as a principal and lead learner. She has served as a special education teacher in grades K–7 and currently serves as an elementary school principal and lead learner at Dunlap Grade School in Dunlap Community Unit School District #323.

Mandy graduated from Bradley University with a bachelor's degree in elementary and special education, a master's degree in curriculum and instruction, and a master's degree in educational leadership and administration.

She has been recognized with several accolades that reaffirm her commitment and dedication to education and leadership. She's been named one of "25 Women in Leadership," "Ten Outstanding Young People in Illinois," Illinois Principals Association Central Illinois Valley Herman Graves Award Winner, and "40 Leaders Under 40." She's earned the Bradley University Graduate Student Leadership and Service Award.

Her biggest accomplishment is her family. She is the proud wife of Brett and mom to Lydia and Lauren. They spend their time "Playing in Peoria" and cheering on the Bradley Braves and Iowa Hawkeyes.

Connect with Mandy:

 @mandyeellis

 @aprincipalsdecree

 PrincipalsDecree.com

CPSIA information can be obtained
at www.ICGtesting.com
Printed in the USA
LVOW13s1138020718
582429LV00055B/982/P